TURNER ON LANDSCAPE

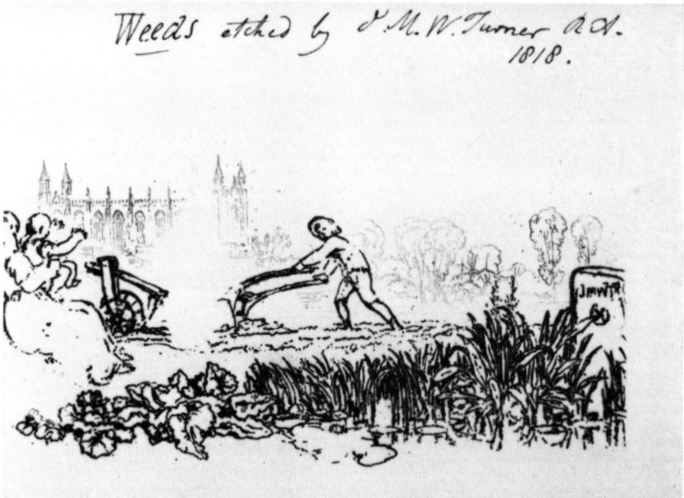

Abandoned etching by Turner for 'Ploughing, Eton' (see page 114)

TURNER ON LANDSCAPE

The *Liber Studiorum*

Gerald Wilkinson

Barrie & Jenkins
LONDON MELBOURNE SYDNEY AUCKLAND JOHANNESBURG

Other books by Gerald Wilkinson

1972: *Turner's Early Sketchbooks 1789–1802*
1974: *The Sketches of Turner, R.A., 1802–20*
1977: *Turner Sketches 1789–1820* (abridged edition of above two titles)
1975: *Turner's Colour Sketches 1820–34*
1982: *A History of Britain's Trees*

Barrie & Jenkins Ltd
An imprint of the Hutchinson Publishing Group
17–21 Conway Street, London W1P 6JD

Hutchinson Group (Australia) Pty Ltd
30–32 Cremorne Street, Richmond South, Victoria 3121
PO Box 151, Broadway, New South Wales 2007

Hutchinson Group (NZ) Ltd
32–34 View Road, PO Box 40–086, Glenfield, Auckland 10

Hutchinson Group (SA) (Pty) Ltd
PO Box 337, Bergvlei 2012, South Africa

First published 1982

Designed by Gerald Wilkinson
Set in Monophoto Garamond
Printed in Great Britain by BAS Printers Limited, Over Wallop, Hampshire
and bound by Wm. Brendon, Tiptree, Essex

ISBN 0 09 144050 5

Contents

Foreword 7

Turner the teacher 10

Liber Studiorum 12

Turner and Claude 15

The drawings for *Liber Studiorum* 23

A note on engraving methods 25

Planning *Liber Studiorum* 28

Engraving *Liber Studiorum* 32

LIBER STUDIORUM Parts 1 to 14

The published plates 41

The engravers of *Liber Studiorum* 111

The unpublished plates 113

Appendix: Turner and the Golden Section 122

Pictorial Index 126

Index 128

ACKNOWLEDGEMENTS

This work was done with generous financial help from Kurt Pantzer of Indianapolis, and his friend Nicholas Noyes. Kurt also lent me essential books from his library, reacted with something like dismay to my theories and demanded an explanation of the Golden Section – this last is appended.

All the illustrations in this book except four are from negatives supplied by the Photographic Section of the British Museum and are reproduced by permission of the Trustees. The exceptions are those illustrations which appear by permission of the Tate Gallery, London (pages 48, below; 93, above); the Walker Art Gallery, Liverpool (page 59, below); and the Museum of Fine Arts, Boston: Francis Bullard Collection (page 117). Thanks to Louella Gwillim for the name of engraving tool no. 12 on page 27, and to Stanley Warburton for reading the proof.

Foreword

Turner was his own publisher for *Liber Studiorum*. He was 32 when the first part came out. He was by then a successful RA and had opened his own gallery in Harley Street. We do not know whether he sought, and failed to find, a publisher for his 'part work'. Boydell, the very successful publisher of Earlom's engravings after Claude's *Liber Veritatis*, was certainly unpopular with the artists – for the obvious reason that he had consistently exploited them. Turner's independent attitude, and the success of the mezzotint engraving of his *Shipwreck* painting of 1805, for which he had a list of 130 subscribers, both suggest that he intended from the first to publish himself.

As the work went on it must have become clear that the publication was going to be only moderately successful, though Turner continued to count the unsold plates at their full value in accounts to be found in a sketchbook (CXXII, 1809–14: '*c.* £2000 probable advantage of Liber Studiorum'). He committed every publishing sin: he was unpredictable in his publication dates; he did very little publicity; and worst of all, he refused a proper commission to printsellers.

After 1819, when publication ceased, the price of a complete set of *Liber Studiorum* was 14 guineas – twice as much for a proof set. The price dropped as low as £3 in the 1840s, according to the first cataloguer, Rawlinson (1878). Charles Turner, the engraver, had many spare proofs which J. M. W. Turner had ordered over the years and not collected, and he used them to light the fire. He had, he said, 'robbed his children of a fortune', for after J. M. W. Turner's death the large stocks of unsold prints in his house were made up into sets which fetched from £300 to £892 each. (The engraved works were sold at Christie's in 1873, having been judged not a part of the Turner Bequest.)

This sudden increase in the value of the *Liber* was no doubt the result of Ruskin's persistent plugging in *Modern Painters* (1843–60) and elsewhere. But clearly, the taste of the English art public, reluctant with the Pre-Raphaelites and blissfully ignorant of the Impressionists, had caught up with 'middle period' Turner.

'Victorian admirers of Turner's *Liber Studiorum*', wrote Finberg in 1924, 'exalted it into something almost superhuman but wholly irrational and incomprehensible'. Perhaps he was thinking of the Reverend Stopford Brooke, who at least attempted some sort of interpretation in a book of reproductions published in 1882 and reprinted in several editions, included a small octavo, during the rest of the century.

In 1878 W. G. Rawlinson published his descriptive catalogue, acknowledging the catalogue of an exhibition of the *Liber* at the Burlington Fine Arts Club in 1872 and freely quoting from the notes and letters of John Pye, the engraver. These last were gathered together in Pye and Roget: *Notes and Memoranda respecting the Liber Studiorum of J. M. W. Turner, RA* (1879).

Cotman made copies of some of Turner's *Liber* plates, probably for his own instruction, and he published his own *Liber Studiorum* in 1838, using soft-ground etching. Frank Short, ARA, re-engraved several of the plates, chosen by Ruskin, from 1886 to 1888.

In about 1910, C. F. Bell, the first and most boring of modern Turner scholars, published a book of reproductions of the *Liber* in an extraordinary sequence. Only the Frontispiece was in more or less the right place, at the front (although chronologically it belongs with Part 10). His text was short and arid.

A. J. Finberg's monumental limited edition, *The History of Turner's Liber Studiorum*, was published in 1924. It is concerned almost entirely with the physical 'states' of the prints and the watermarks of the various papers used, but it has accurate transcriptions of lettering, etc. There is not a word of any sort of interpretation of Turner's meaning and, surprisingly for so large a work, no bibliography. All the drawings, etchings, and published and unpublished plates are reproduced, in dull but accurate collotype, the text being overprinted in fine letterpress. Only 650 numbered copies were issued (at, I believe, £3.10s.).

Nobody since the redoubtable (and very fanciful) Stopford Brooke has attempted any complete commentary on the plates themselves. In 1975 Luke Hermann wrote: 'Turner's aim was to display his mastery and versatility in the most popular traditional and contemporary modes of landscape and marine painting.' Well, marine painting was popular, but history painting was more so than landscape; and Turner displayed his mastery to his fellow Academicians in his painting, not to the general public in his engravings.

Butlin and Wilton, in the catalogue of the 1975 Centenary Exhibition at Burlington House (Tate Gallery Publications, 1974), are closer to the truth about the *Liber*. 'It was conceived from the first as a kind of visual treatise on landscape art, and is the central document of Turner the theorist of painting.' I had not read this remark when I began the present work, but it exactly echoes my conclusion.

We may still experience, as I did at first, and as Ruskin describes, a certain antipathy to the style of the engravings, rooted as it is in the distant world of early nineteenth-century art. There were no mechanical reproductions then, in monochrome or colour, and brown was very fashionable. When I first looked at the *Liber* plates, I must admit I was discouraged. Later, when I had studied all Turner's drawings for *The Sketches of Turner, R.A. 1802–20*, I found myself hooked. It was hard to leave this fascinating period of Turner's life: his astonishing ambitions and equally astonishing triumphs against the all-too-human background of Academy rivalries and politics – and his mysterious personal life with Sarah Danby. I started to study the *Liber* and, perhaps identifying in some way with the master, began to see some of its meanings.

Originally I envisaged this book in a very large format with the five plates of each part on a single page. Later the present format was arrived at, and while we cannot see all the plates of each part together, there is the advantage of a reasonable amount of space round each plate, as Turner planned.

Turner the teacher

Sir Edwin Landseer, who was born in 1802, the year that Turner became a Royal Academician, said in 1863 that Turner was 'without exception . . . the best teacher I have ever met with . . . he was thoroughly grounded in everything'.

No-one is surprised to hear that a painter is also a teacher: the tradition is at least as old as the Renaissance. Equally, it is not surprising when a successful artist gives up his teaching. But Turner, always successful in spite of continuous barracking by the critics, was a teacher all his life, by choice. He became the Academy's Professor of Perspective, and he did his stint with the others – Etty for instance – in the Life Academy. As a young man he had some private pupils – amateurs – and at least one of his patrons later in life went abroad with him on sketching trips, as did the rich amateur, Munro of Novar, in 1836. But his best teaching was done by example, and it was this that Landseer remembered; though he did say, also, that 'whatever he suggested, was done without question, and it was always an improvement'.

Such exchanges took place on the Academy Varnishing Days, three or more, which had been allowed since 1809 for members to touch up their pictures after they had been hung. There was, no doubt, an atmosphere of free discussion among the Academicians, relaxed after their winters' labours. There was much friendly rivalry, which the newspapers' gossip columns insisted was not so friendly on Turner's part – he was often accused of deliberately outshining another painter by supposedly excessive use of white or colour.

In the 1830s and 40s Turner was unique in that he often hung paintings that were barely half-finished, so that his work on the three to six Varnishing Days – he called them 'painting days' – was a virtuoso display of his techniques and a subtle demonstration of his principles of design. Few people can resist watching an artist build up his picture, and the Royal Academicians were no exceptions.

Robert Leslie, the son of C. R. Leslie, RA, described Turner on his painting days:

> His colours were usually taken from small gallipots or old teacups [he reputedly used a palette loaded only with white], which stood on a stool beside him when he was at work. Turner's pictures when first hung upon the

> walls were almost devoid of colour and detail . . . Upon these ghostlike effects as they hung in his massive old tarnished frames, Turner worked, standing from six in the morning until dark, and dividing his time among them as inclination led him, during the six varnishing days which were then allotted to the Royal Academicians.

This was Turner aged about 60. After his death the Varnishing Days were reduced in number. (He died in 1851, aged 76.)

Ruskin described Turner as he appeared to the young admirer who was to become his great commentator:

> Everyone had described him to me as coarse, boorish, unintellectual, vulgar. This I knew to be impossible. I found in him a somewhat eccentric, keen-mannered, matter-of-fact, English-minded gentleman: good natured evidently, bad tempered evidently, hating humbug of all sorts, shrewd, perhaps a little selfish, highly intellectual, the powers of his mind not brought out with any delight in their manifestation, or intention of display, but flashing out occasionally in a word or a look.

These qualities are not perhaps those of a typical teacher, though they could be those of a great teacher. As a young man he must have been even more bluff, and his manners were awkward. Edward Dayes wrote in 1804: 'The man must be loved for his works, for his person is not striking, or his conversation brilliant.'* However, Turner's fellow Academicians, as practical painters, were not put off by superficialities. At the age of 32 he was voted by twenty-seven to one into the newly created post of Professor of Perspective. He *was* the only candidate, but even so his fellows must have been in no doubt of his ability. His duties, which consisted of an annual series of lectures, he took very seriously: but he was, it appears, largely unintelligible. In many years he failed to give the lectures at all, though it is clear from his notes and illustrations that they were very well prepared. He loved to sign himself RAPP, and this he did on many plates of *Liber Studiorum*.

Firmly attached as Turner was to the Royal Academy, its Schools and its annual Exhibitions, he had begun to plan his own gallery, and, in the year before he became a Professor, his own book on landscape composition. It was to be a manifesto without words and a demonstration of the expressive power and scope of landscape in art.

*Dayes was Girtin's master. He was, said Edward Edwards (Turner's Teacher of Perspective at the Academy), of a temper 'neither amiable nor happy'.

Liber Studiorum

J. M. W. Turner, RAPP, began to publish in 1807, at his own expense, a series of engravings 'illustrative of landscape compositions'. His subtitle continues: 'viz. Historical, Mountainous, Pastoral, Marine and Architectural'.

That was all anyone was ever told about the purpose of the *Liber*. There was no text. Turner was never communicative about his own work (and he rarely commented on that of his contemporaries).

The title and the style of the engravings were based on an influential precedent: the engravings by Richard Earlom after Claude's *Liber Veritatis*.

Turner's engravings, like Earlom's, are in mezzotint on copper, about 7 × 10 inches (18 × 25 cm). Again like Earlom's, they were printed in dark brown.

There were fourteen parts and each part contained five plates. This fact is important, for the plates will usually be seen displayed in separate frames, and have always been *discussed* separately. I believe that Turner intended each published part to form a concise chapter of his book, although he did not number the plates.

The plates were printed on sheets of French Auvergne paper watermarked 'T Dupuy' up to Part 4, and English paper by Whatman or H. Smith from Parts 5 to 10. Parts 11 and 12, published after the Napoleonic Wars, returned to French paper made by T. Richard. The size of the sheet appears to have been Colombier, trimmed into four pieces, according to Finberg.* The prints were stitched into blue, sugar-paper folders bearing the title (set in the latest fat-faced Roman type) and the author's signature. The size of the folder was about 11 × 15 inches (28 × 38 cm) or imperial quarto, 'landscape'.

Each plate carried an inscription in the manner of engravings at the time: usually a title, credits for artist and engraver, and details of date (usually) and place of publication. Nineteen of the seventy published designs were based on existing paintings or drawings. Of these, ten were attributed in the inscription to various patrons, three were in the possession of the artist, and so inscribed, while the remaining six were based on paintings but not so described.

**The History of Turner's Liber Studiorum*, 1924.

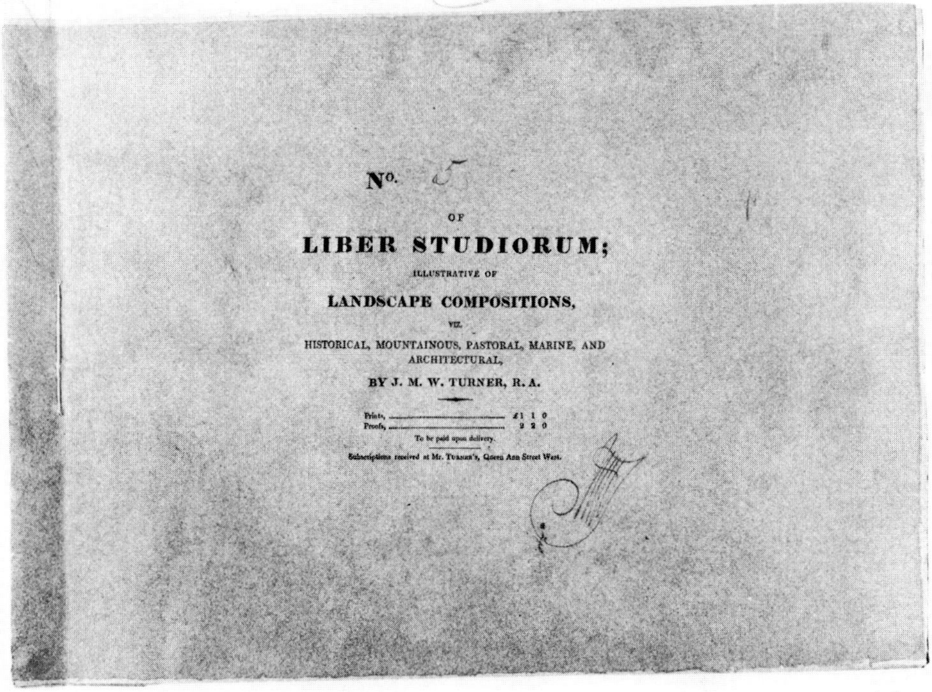

The blue paper cover of Part 5 of *Liber Studiorum*

At the head of each plate was engraved a simple letter:

P for Pastoral (often a genre subject, always contemporary)

EP taken to mean Epic or Elevated Pastoral* (often classical in the Claude tradition, but not always)

M or Ma usually, but not always, a 'sea piece'

A for Architectural: ruins, townscapes and one interior of a church

M or Ms for Mountainous

H for Historical, in fact always biblical or mythological

Publication was sporadic up to 1819, when it ceased – sometimes two parts came out in one year, sometimes there was a gap of up to three years. Of the hundred plates originally intended, seventy were actually issued plus a Frontispiece included in Part 10. Twenty plates were left uncompleted, and the final ten

*The meaning of these initials is not explained anywhere in Turner's notes, so it is uncertain. He used the term 'elevated' in his lectures, and in a letter, 1811, in the sense of 'on a more elevated plane of thought than the everyday'. He wished to distinguish between what we might call 'rural genre' and landscapes-with-figures in the classical manner of Poussin and Claude – 'elevated pastorals'.

can be rather doubtfully identified amongst Turner's drawings.* He produced working drawings in sepia for most of the plates, and these are preserved in the British Museum Print Room.

In addition Turner worked experimentally on twelve slightly smaller mezzotint plates, soon after work on *Liber Studiorum* ceased. These are sometimes called the 'Little Liber'.

The first part or number was priced at 15 shillings ('Proofs 1.15*s*'). The prices were increased two years later to 1 guinea, and 2 guineas for proof copies. According to a note in one of Turner's pocket books (the Hastings sketchbook, Turner Bequest CXI, pp. 96a and 97a) he had a hundred subscribers in 1810. He printed twenty 'proofs'. Most of the plates needed a considerable amount of retouching to produce more than about thirty prints of acceptable quality, but Turner was less fastidious than his collectors have proved to be. Also, he made use of the opportunity of reworking to make interesting modifications in his designs. 'He repaired the plates again and again,' wrote Pye, one of his engravers, 'but he never again reinserted on the margins of the plates the letters which were necessary to enable the public to distinguish proof from print impressions.'

Copies were obtainable only from the artist, or, in the case of the earlier parts, from his engraver. No attempt was made to find other means of distribution – or at least, according to Pye, 'the allowance he made to print-sellers for dealing in it was so much under that which they required, that the *Liber Studiorum* was never fairly placed before the world'. Pye was writing in 1852.

No serious attempt was made to advertise the early parts. A prospectus, handwritten, was displayed in Turner's gallery in Harley Street, along with some of the drawings for the series. It proposed publishing 'one hundred landscapes, to be designed and etched by J. M. W. Turner, RA, and engraved in Mezzotinto'.

*See Rawlinson, *Turner's Liber Studiorum*, 1906.

Turner and Claude

Claude Lorrain compiled his *Liber Veritatis* over a period of nearly fifty years. He began his book, which finally contained 195 copies of his paintings, as a record of his work and a protection against plagiarism. The drawings contain a good deal of detail and were inscribed on the reverse with a number, the name of the client or just where the picture had been sent, and sometimes the date.

As the work gradually built up, Claude began to treat it as a work of art in itself, and in subtle ways made the drawings more expressive, even adding colour to the basic near-monochrome pen and wash.

From about 1720 *Liber Veritatis* was in the collection of the Dukes of Devonshire. From 1774 to 1777 a series of mezzotints 'in the manner and taste of the drawings', engraved by Richard Earlom, was published in London by Boydell. Claude's *Liber* was transformed from a private record of his compositions (his '*libro d'invenzione*') that very few people had seen, into a best-selling art book which could be taken as a guide to classical landscape composition.

Earlom etched the line-work before adding a mezzotint ground and scraping to produce the effect of broad washes over a pen line. 'This use of etching,' says Arthur Hayden in *Chats on Old Prints*, 'had by this time become universal in mezzotint.' If so – and the point is questionable – it is well concealed in the work of one of the greatest engravers in mezzotint, John Raphael Smith (1752–1812). The technique certainly suited Earlom's purpose. The total effect of his work, published in two folio volumes in 1777, is lively: the brown, matt ink glows golden in the light tones of Claude's sunsets, and richly dark in his bosky shades. But the engraver, in attempting with his needle to imitate the masterly speed of Claude's pen, exposed the weakness of his own draughtsmanship. The plates of Earlom's *Liber Veritatis* are really very inferior versions of the originals – but, somehow, 200 years later, their crudity is forgivable. It was a noble effort; and engraved reproductions usually fail through cowardly niggling, not from excessive *brio*.

Turner was generally supposed to have modelled his *Liber Studiorum* on the 1777 *Liber Veritatis*. A famous letter from Clara Wheeler (to a Mr Elliot in 1853) uses the phrase, 'on the plan of the *Liber Veritatis*'. Clara was the daughter of

W. F. Wells, the watercolourist, a great friend of Turner's youth. According to his daughter, Wells persuaded Turner to embark on his *Liber*, planned the size of the plates and arranged the subjects of the first number. This last is unlikely, but certainly the friends may have discussed it, by the fireside of Wells's cottage at Knockholt in Kent, perhaps in the autumn of 1806. A sketchbook of that year, in Sussex, shows two well-worked-out compositions that did not appear in the *Liber* until 1812 and 1819.* Turner's plan continued to take shape in his mind, obviously, after his talk with Wells, and it remained there as he collected and reshuffled his subjects, occasionally making lists of them in his notebooks (Finberg gave the titles '*Liber* Notes 1 and 2', and 'Studies for *Liber*' to three of the sketchbooks in the Turner Bequest).† The true shape of his plan emerges, however, not from the artist's casual jottings, but from a study of the book itself. It has always been seen as an *ad hoc* collection. Collectors, most of whom seem to be concerned only with surface qualities, unique states, and so on, tend to increase this fragmentation.

Clara Wheeler was only a few years younger than Turner. She recorded that he loved her father 'with a son's affection', and she remained friendly with him for most of his life, so she is not likely to have got her facts far wrong. 'It seems but yesterday,' she wrote, 'tho' fifty years are passed and gone.' Turner's visits were 'one scene of fun and merriment'. The Turner who conceived *Liber Studiorum* was young, successful, wiry and energetic, and inspired; and the nineteenth century was only six years old.

Because Turner was ambitious – for himself, for landscape art (his chosen field), for British art – and had, later, the temerity to set his own paintings beside the work of Claude, the phrase 'rivalry with Claude' came to be repeated by every Victorian writer about the *Liber* (except Ruskin, who knew better). Claude's position, amongst amateurs and landscapists of the late eighteenth century, however, was unassailable; but his name was mentioned more than any other artist in the newspaper criticisms of the early nineteenth century, when Turner was making his reputation. The critics, when they were pleased with him, said he combined the best of Claude with the best of Wilson; and these two were certainly Turner's early heroes.

*Reproduced in Wilkinson, 1974.
†*Inventory of the Drawings in the Turner Bequest,* 1909.

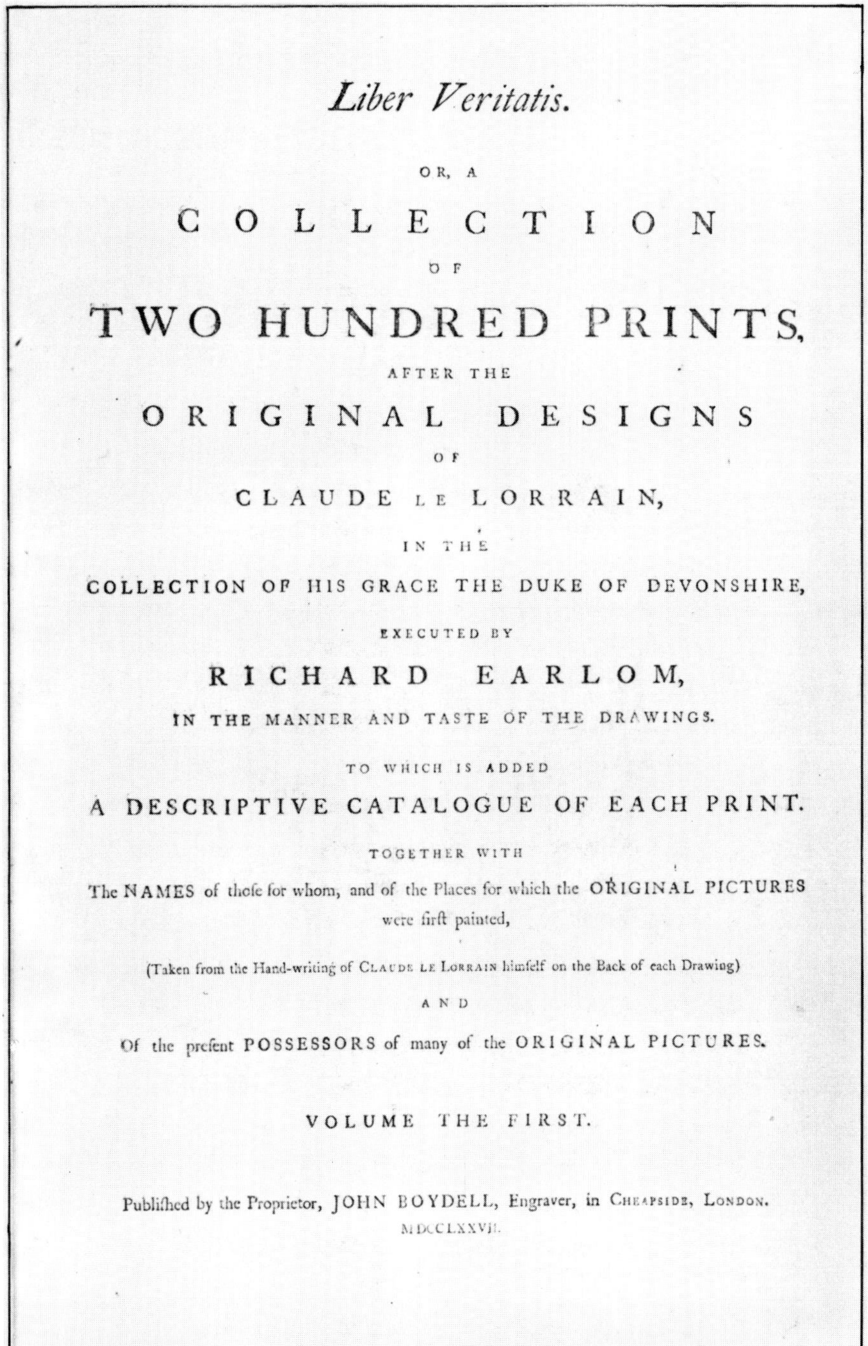

Liber Veritatis.

OR, A

COLLECTION

OF

TWO HUNDRED PRINTS,

AFTER THE

ORIGINAL DESIGNS

OF

CLAUDE LE LORRAIN,

IN THE

COLLECTION OF HIS GRACE THE DUKE OF DEVONSHIRE,

EXECUTED BY

RICHARD EARLOM,

IN THE MANNER AND TASTE OF THE DRAWINGS.

TO WHICH IS ADDED

A DESCRIPTIVE CATALOGUE OF EACH PRINT.

TOGETHER WITH

The NAMES of thoſe for whom, and of the Places for which the ORIGINAL PICTURES were firſt painted,

(Taken from the Hand-writing of CLAUDE LE LORRAIN himſelf on the Back of each Drawing)

AND

Of the preſent POSSESSORS of many of the ORIGINAL PICTURES.

VOLUME THE FIRST.

Publiſhed by the Proprietor, JOHN BOYDELL, Engraver, in CHEAPSIDE, LONDON.

MDCCLXXVII.

Title page of the 1777 *Liber Veritatis*

Turner venerated Claude. In his lecture, first delivered in 1811, *Backgrounds: Introduction of architecture and landscape*, Turner's plodding, struggling sentences seem to take wings of unusual eloquence:

> Pure as Italian air, calm, beautiful and serene, spring forward the works and the name of Claude Lorrain. The golden orient or the amber-coloured ether, the midday ethereal vault; the fleecy skies, resplendent valleys, campagnas rich with all the cheerful blush of fertility, trees possessing every hue and tone of summer's heat; rich, harmonious, true and clear, replete with all the aerial qualities of distance (aerial lights, aerial colour) – where, through all these comprehensive qualities and powers, can we find a clue to his mode of practice?*

– only through 'continual study of the parts of nature', concludes the Professor of Perspective. It was a lesson he had learnt well himself.

Turner knew several of Claude's paintings in the original – 'The choicest of his works are with us,' he remarked in his lecture, 'and may they always remain in this country.' His youthful reaction to one of them, *Sacrifice to Apollo*, had been recorded by Farington in his *Diary*† (May 1799): 'He was both pleased and unhappy while he viewed it; it seemed to be beyond the power of imitation.'

In 1819, as he journeyed to Rome, Turner noted, at Loretto, 'the first bit of Claude' (sketchbook CLXXVII, p. 6). The name alone was a term of praise in Turner's shorthand – even, with unconscious humour, praise of an Italian cow: 'dun brown, Claude' (CLXXVI, p. 22a). Claude's frequent depiction of the disc of the sun in his evening landscapes may have been the origin of Turner's obsession with the sun, his frequent use of the light source at the centre of his compositions – and indeed his lifelong study of sunrises and sunsets.

Turner's devotion to Claude lasted from an early age right through the period of the *Liber*. His bequest of his favourite *Carthage* picture and a seascape to the National Gallery, 'provided they are deemed worthy to be and are placed by the side of Claude's *Seaport* and *Mill*', must be seen as an aspect of that devotion. This part of his will was made in 1829.

His rivalry, if any, was with Earlom's publisher, Boydell – as Finberg points

*From Jerrold Ziff, 'A lecture by J. M. W. Turner', *Journal of the Warburg and Courtauld Institutes*, vol. 26, 1963. I have added some punctuation, because even Turner must have taken a breath here and there.

†*The Farington Diary*, ed. Grieg, 1922.

out. Boydell had done very well out of publishing prints, and he was unpopular with the artists. The engraver, Landseer, was so obsessed with dislike of Boydell that he could not resist making a personal attack during a course of lectures at the British Institution – and was promptly dismissed by the managers. This was in 1806, the very year in which, in October, Wells and Turner were planning the great project. Turner intended to have no truck with publishers and printsellers.

The plan of the work and the style of presentation, then, were to be modelled on the engraved version of *Liber Veritatis* and published as engravings perhaps in competition with, certainly in a manner similar to, the Boydell *Collection of Prints* (to give the book its proper title). There the similarity ends; or would end, were it not that Earlom had progressed to a further volume of Claude engravings.

Of the reproductions in the 1777 *Liber Veritatis* Basil Gray (*The English Print*) says: 'Turner regarded these prints with disgust, as travesties of the originals at Chatsworth' – which, of course, leads us to ask two questions: how does Gray know Turner's feelings, and had the artist seen the Claudes in the Devonshire Collection? *Liber Veritatis* was in London until 1835 but hardly accessible. There were Claude drawings in every good collection, however – the painter Lawrence, with whom Turner was usually on good terms, had a hundred at one time. Turner's feelings about Earlom's work may have been as described, though not perhaps descending to disgust. Artists at this time had no 'good' reproductions: they must have been used to interpreting the classics of painting through the variable skills of engravers.

However, from 1803 onwards Earlom had been producing a new series of Claude reproductions, much more impressive than the first two volumes in both technique and variety of content. There can be no doubt that Turner and his friends collected these prints and talked about them, perhaps even forgetting the somewhat monotonous volumes published twenty-six years before. The so-called Third Volume of *Liber Veritatis* included a few stragglers from the Devonshire Collection but it ranged much more widely amongst all Claude's drawings and included many drawings from nature. Some of these, as the reproduction here may show, were quite skilfully interpreted in the engravings. The pattern set by Earlom's third volume is close to Turner's plan, which was to draw on his exhibited work but largely to use his sketches and his imagination for the plates of *Liber Studiorum*.

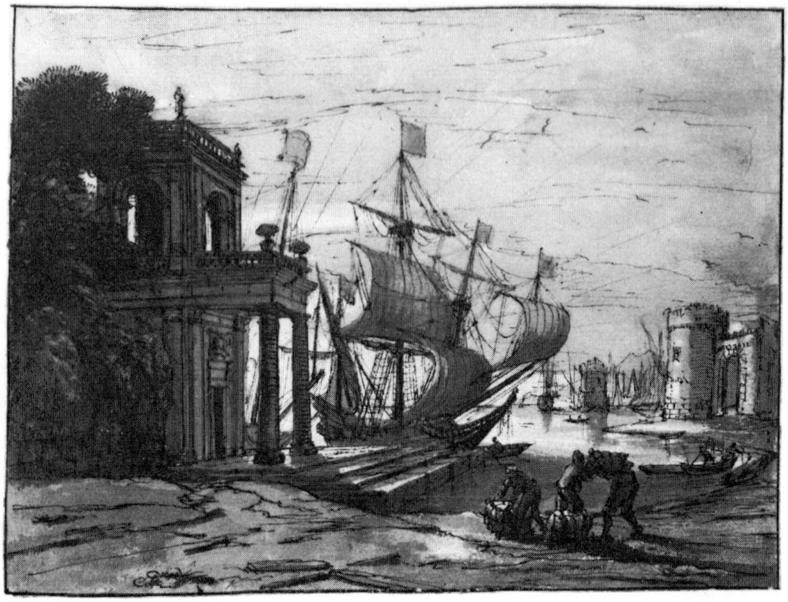

Claude's sepia drawing of his picture *per Turino*, now unknown

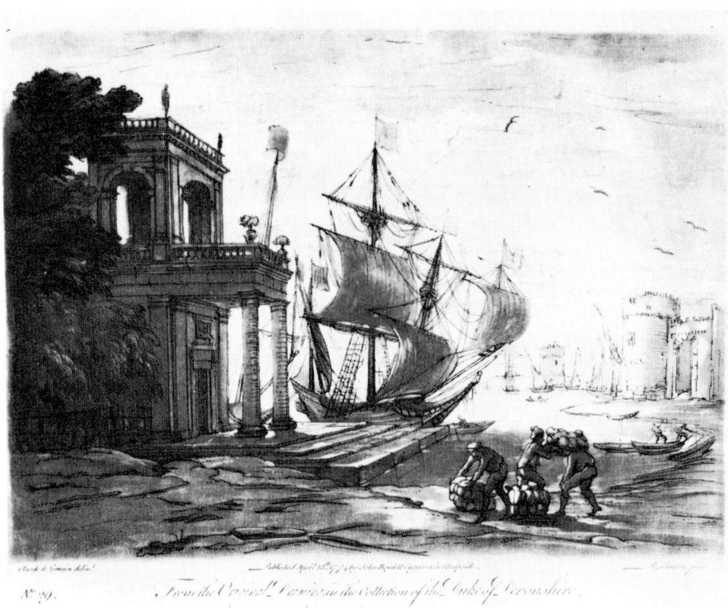

Engraving by Earlom after Claude: no. 29 of *Liber Veritatis*

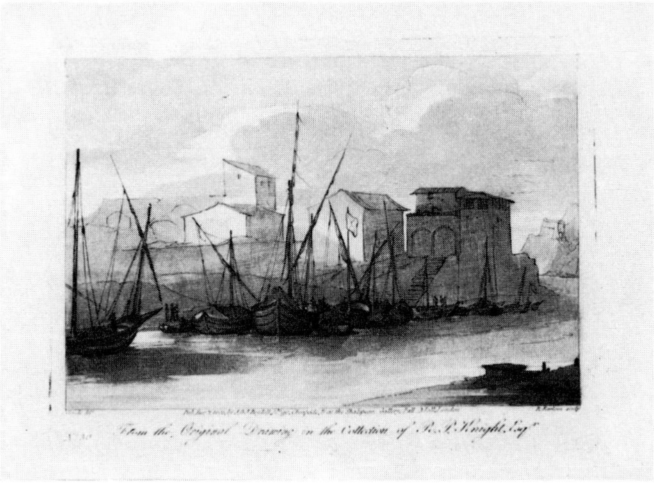

Engraving by Earlom from the so-called Third Volume of *Liber Veritatis*

Studiorum: of studies; of the studio; for study? Perhaps all three were in the mind of the artist, who knew as much Latin as I do. Turner clearly intended to follow the *Veritatis* technique of line and tone in sepia-coloured ink. He produced working drawings in sepia pen and wash, reinterpreting his own work for the format of the *Liber*, as well as working out new compositions. He promised himself, in a draft advertisement, to exhibit as many as fifty of these drawings in 1808, in the gallery attached to his house. We do not know whether, on the day, he showed that many (he had already published fifteen) but obviously the enthusiasm was there. For the next few years his sketchbooks were full of ideas and notes for the *Liber* subjects.

It was important to Turner, I believe, that the five pictures in each part should be seen as a group (and they are so displayed in this volume). He often repeated, about his work, 'What use is it, except together?' – indeed, this is why we have a Turner Bequest. There is a story that when he found some plates of the *Liber* on sale separately, he exclaimed: 'A pack of geese! Don't they know what "Liber Studiorum" means?'

This insistence, that the single work is only part of the dynamic whole, is surely the very stuff that art historians feed on. It is unusual in an artist. Turner had a strong dramatic and literary sense, wholly frustrated in his personal bearing and utterances, but always present in his designing and painting. It was an undertone of hidden meanings, allusion, symbolism and poetry. His work lives in a world between painting and illustration – though it is not divided. He was the most aware of artists – a great builder of bridges in the mind (as I think he tells us in the first part of the *Liber*). He was a leaper over abysses and a flier over vast distances. But here we are only at the beginning. At a time when many artists were publishing systems or methods of composition, Turner produced, not a 'method', but a silent sequence of reminders of the immense diversity of expression which he saw in landscape. English landscape painting, in Turner's early days, was only just beginning to be taken seriously by the Academics. Wilson and Gainsborough had both, sadly, found landscape unprofitable.

He loved to have a series to work on, as we know from many examples; this was the first to mature: all his own ideas to be poured into a single mould, for distribution to the eager subscribers. But they, and he, were wearied before it was completed – or so we have been led to believe. Certainly his business methods worked against him, and the engraved results are far from representing his finest work of the period. But we do well to look beyond the sometimes slightly unpleasant surface and the occasional banality to the underlying beauty and grandeur of the conception. There are, also, many great moments.

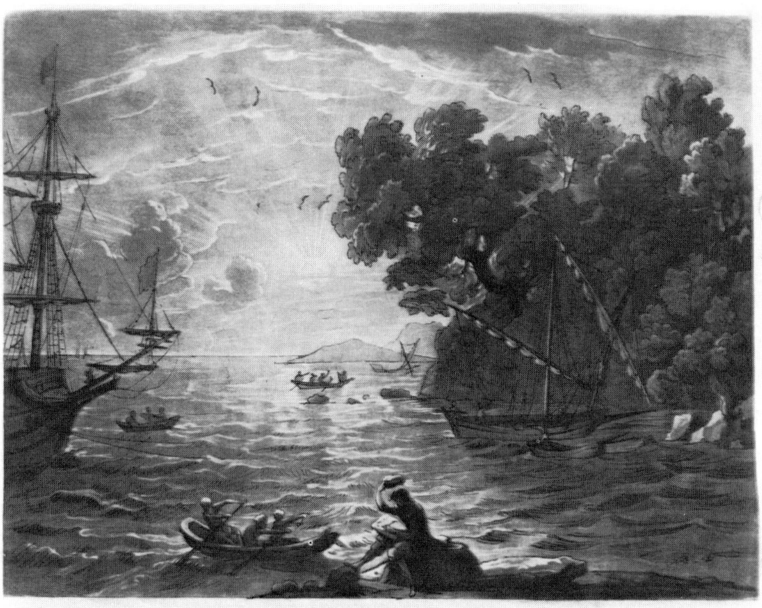

No. 130 of *Liber Veritatis*, engraved by Earlom

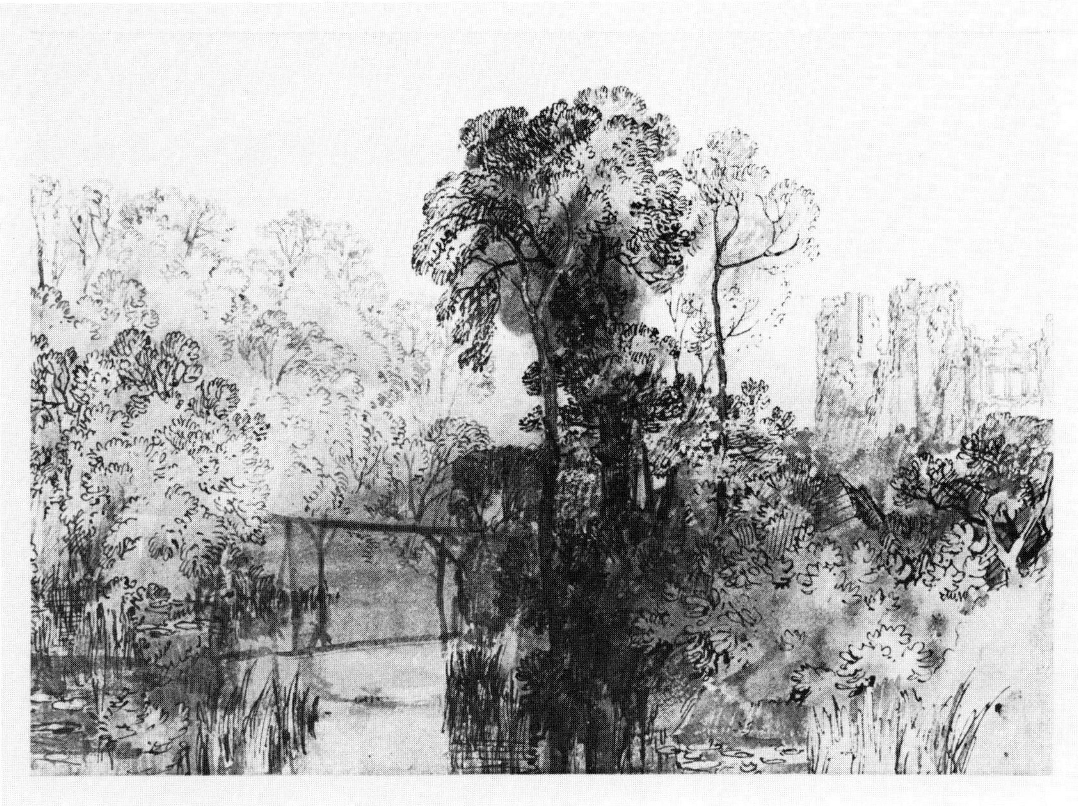

Berry Pomeroy

The drawings for *Liber Studiorum*

Eighty-three drawings in pen and brown wash are part of the Turner Bequest now in the Print Room at the British Museum: Turner Bequest CXVI to CXVIII. Unlike the drawings for Turner's later published series, the *Liber* drawings are obviously cartoons for the engravings. They are clear and simple (relatively), and the tones are laid down with deliberation and closely keyed with the line-work. In the earlier drawings, say before 1810, the line clings cautiously to the main tonal masses which in the engravings it will have to support. There is nothing of Turner's later, celebrated 'indistinctness'. Above all, they are in monochrome.

In the more advanced *Liber* drawings, such as the beautiful 'Berry Pomeroy Castle', the line is free. It plays a virtuoso part in the composition. Line and wash interpenetrate; they work together and separately, now combining, now falling delicately apart, and sometimes playfully each taking up the function of the other. This is the true relationship of line with brushwork, and in rediscovering it (he knew it well enough in his sketchbooks), Turner came close to the spirit of Claude.

In his *History of Turner's Liber Studiorum*, published in 1924, Finberg provides complex evidence for believing that sixty-seven of the drawings were made between 1806 and 1810, proposing this 'comparatively short period' to have been responsible for what he sees as the unity of character of the series. This unity is, I feel, more a function of the format for which the artist was working than a factual reality. Finberg's estimate of time and motion ignores the distance that Turner could travel in a single day, if so inspired, even within this restricted framework.

Look again at the drawing for 'Berry Pomeroy' or the one for *Mill near the Grand Chartreuse*.* Compare them with the plates of the same subjects (Plates 58 and 54). No more need be said. But here we are concerned with the plates for the qualities they do contain.

The drawings for *Liber Studiorum* form a consistent body of work and are certainly close to Turner's conception of his illustrations of landscape composition. They were working drawings, intended to be followed by the mezzotint engravers (who sometimes complained that Turner, in etching the line-work, had not followed his own designs).

There would be some argument for reproducing the drawings here instead of the engravings, but I have rejected this idea because after all, Turner's object was to produce a printed book. Also, the prints are collectable and this volume is intended to be of use to collectors, who, even if they only have one *Liber* plate, come nearer than many of us to possessing a real Turner, and may, I hope, see their possession in a fresh light.

*Wilkinson, 1974, p. 116.

A note on engraving methods

Any reader who practises engraving should ignore these pages: he will not learn anything and will probably disagree with the wording of these brief descriptions based on early nineteenth-century practice.

All the processes described are printed by the intaglio method. Intaglio properly means the engraving of an image in 'reverse relief' – the opposite of 'cameo'. The heated plate is inked and wiped clean on the surface, all the ink being forced into the engraved lines and dots. It is then polished on the surface, to remove all the ink from the lightest parts, and printed under great pressure in a roller press. The pressure, through felt blankets, forces the paper into the declivities of the engraving so that most of the ink held there is transferred.

Etching is the process of drawing with a needle into hard wax varnish covering a metal plate, the plate being then immersed in a solution of nitric acid (aquafortis) which bites into the parts not covered with varnish. The biting is repeated; lines required to print faintly are stopped out with varnish while those required to be strong are etched deeper (and will become thicker).

A plate of soft metal can be etched by *dry-point* – that is, without the use of acid. Plates etched or engraved by other means may have the addition of dry-point etching. The needle used is heavier and sharper than an etching needle; it may be tipped with diamond. The lines thus scratched on the plate have a characteristic burr which holds the ink, but they are shallow, and dry-point soon wears in printing.

In *soft-ground etching* a drawing may be traced from thin paper on to the plate, which is grounded with varnish to which a critical amount of lard has been added. A lead pencil or a blunt needle may be used to trace the design through. Wherever it is touched, the paper lifts the ground from the plate, exposing the metal. Even the texture of a laid paper can be reproduced. The plate is bitten as described above, the printed result resembling a fine chalk drawing.

In *line engraving*,* the pure use of the graver, otherwise known as the burin, cuts the design on polished metal – copper until the introduction of steel in the

*The term is now used for the making of relief blocks, without half-tones, for printing by letterpress.

early 1820s. The design must be built up entirely by parallel lines, cross-hatching and dots. The burin cuts, or ploughs, a V-section into the metal, throwing up a burr at the sides and a spike at the end of the stroke. These are sheared off. Unwanted fine lines and scratches can be burnished out, but for large corrections the surface of the plate must be raised from the back and repolished.

In the early nineteenth century an 'engraver's etching' consisted of the main lines and sometimes the darkest parts of an engraving, intended to be completed by other means, bitten in by acid. This preliminary stage was not an essential part of engraving, but its use had become habitual in England in Turner's time. His etchings for *Liber Studiorum* are engraver's etchings, but, unusually, they are autographic.

The eighteenth-century 'crayon manner' employed various roulettes and stippling tools, and sometimes etching, to match in line engraving the irregular pattern of fine dots produced by drawing with crayon or chalk. A more regular and even pattern of fine dots was used to reproduce smooth, 'stumped' chalk drawings, and this method developed into a technique of *stipple engraving*, using dots applied by roulette and burin to represent the continuous tones of paintings – usually flattening detail and texture in a way unacceptable to the more fastidious craftsmen and collectors.

In *mezzotint* a very fine roughened texture is made on the plate by the systematic use of a rocker tool with a serrated, curved edge. The final, textured ground prints solid black. Half-tones are produced by scraping down the textured surface to varying degrees, burnishing to remove the marks of the scraper, and polishing smooth the areas that are to print lightest. The engraver is thus working from dark to light.

Aquatint is a form of etching in which flat tones are produced by the acid biting through a porous ground, usually made by half-melting powdered resin on to the metal. The name refers to its early use in simulating watercolour washes. Aquatint can be combined with lines previously etched, but there is a tendency for the ground to 'stand away' from the lines. If the line is etched after the aquatint it bites unevenly. Subtle variations of tone, and gradations, are difficult; but the process of aquatinting is a comparatively rapid one. Aquatint was often used for light, flat tones in mezzotints and also was sometimes applied to mezzotint areas which had been made too light by mistake.

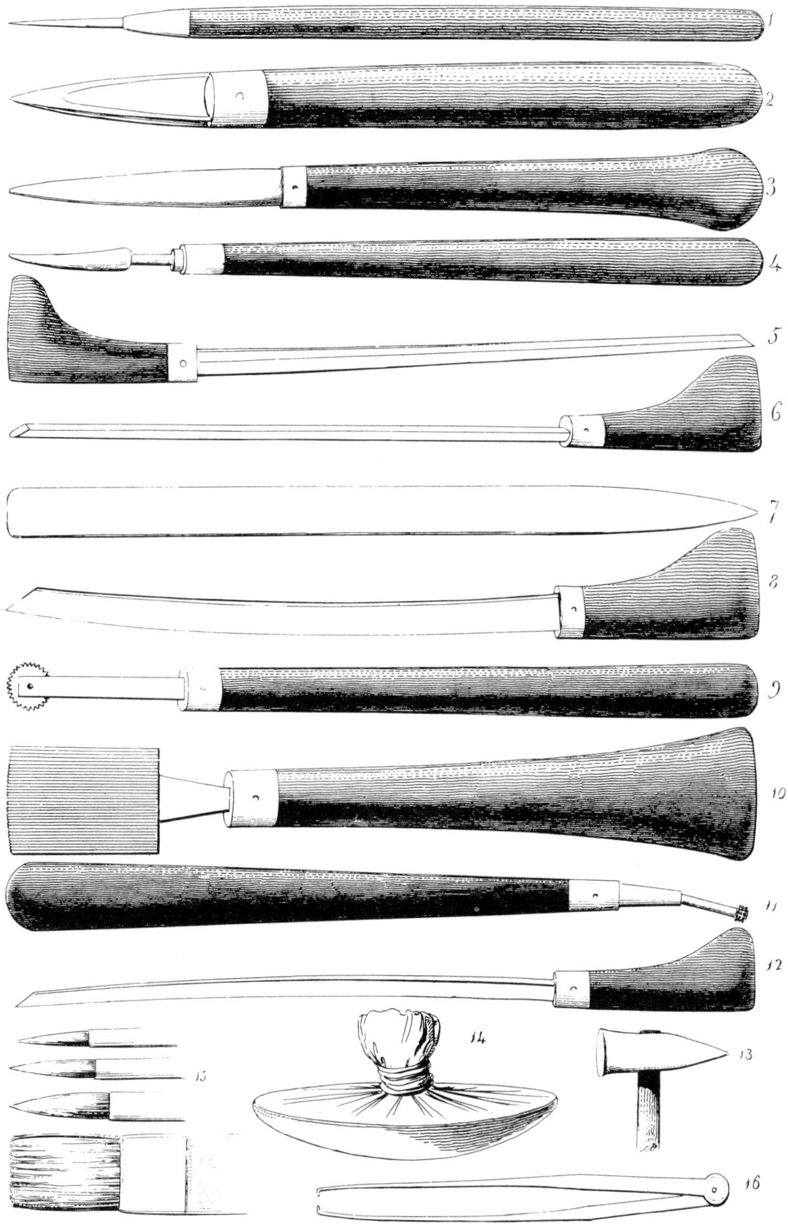

From Fielding, *Art of Engraving*, 1844

1 etching needle
2 scraper for taking off the burr
3 burnisher, to soften lines which have been bit too dark
4 mezzotinter's burnisher, for all neat and delicate work
5 (and 8?) graver
6 'scooper'
7 scraper
9 roulette for lines
10 shading tool
11 roulette for darkening
12 stippling tool
13 polished steel anvil
14 dabber, to lay etching grounds
15 camel's hair brushes, for sweeping off loose varnish, stopping out, laying grounds etc
16 caliper compasses

Planning *Liber Studiorum*

London in the young Turner's day was the home of mezzotint engraving – *la manière anglaise* or *manière noire* (a German name was *Schwarzkunst* – black art). It was almost entirely reproductive; that is, few works were designed for the process and probably none was conceived as a mezzotint. When an engraver wished to publish his own work he would first execute a painting and then engrave it 'after' himself.

Late eighteenth-century mezzotints of paintings, frequently of portraits, are remarkable for accuracy and high finish; they come close to being 'photographic' – with a certain quality that could never come through the lens. Though perhaps somewhat sooty and opaque, they are large and very decorative. Mezzotint prints were often coloured by hand – not very successfully, for of course every tint had to blend with black.

Aquatint was less esteemed. It was comparatively new: Le Prince, a pupil of Boucher, first used the process in about 1770, and Paul Sandby took it up in England, establishing a tradition of topographical aquatint. Aquatint was valued for the way it could be used to imitate watercolour washes – hence its name – though its shortcomings were well known. John Landseer* sneered at Gilpin's 'smearings' – but Turner as a boy was not above copying from Gilpin, as is proved by two drawings identified by Finberg but now apparently missing from the Print Room at the British Museum.

Aquatint was much used, in the early nineteenth century, as a basis for hand-colouring – by teams of women, each applying one colour, in true mass-production style. Ackermann was the famous publisher of many such prints, notably the vigorous productions of Rowlandson. Thomas Malton, the excellent architectural draughtsman who was Turner's early teacher, produced most of his work in aquatint which was crisp and accurate and made no attempt to simulate the free brushwork of watercolour.

The engravers, artists and publishers at the turn of the century were curiously divided and illogical in their attitude to the various print processes. The need to publish was compelling to some artists (of whom Turner was evidently one and

***Lectures on the Art of Engraving*, 1807.

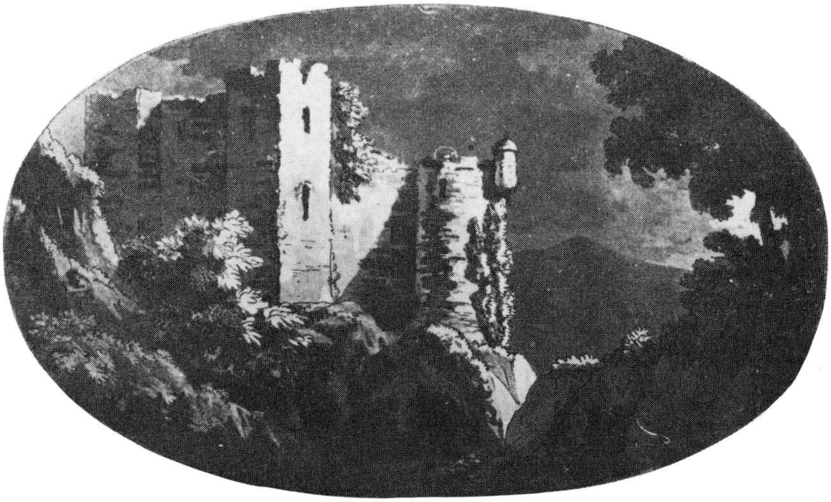

Aquatinted plate from Gilpin

William Blake certainly another), and the demand for reproductions of all kinds was obviously strong. But the arts of reproduction seem to have been governed very much by prejudice and convention. Engravers were many, but they were a lower class of being than painters.

The Academicians on the whole preferred to leave engraving to the mere craftsmen: when they accepted illustration commissions they produced paintings or drawings and left it to the engravers to sort out the reproduction problems – a form of lofty artistic incompetence not unknown even today. The RA excluded a fine draughtsman like Malton from even associateship (on the grounds, as noted by Farington, that he only drew what other men had designed), while including the sentimental painter Angelica Kauffman, who was in fact a best-seller on the print stalls.

Stipple engraving was the most popular form at the end of the eighteenth century, especially from the hand of Bartolozzi and his pupils. (Francesco Bartolozzi, 1727–1815, was a founder member of the Royal Academy, but he was included as a painter, not as an engraver.) Stipple engravings were cheap to produce – only about a third of the cost of line engravings – for they could be worked more quickly and with inexpert assistance. The related 'chalk manner' was used for reproducing drawings; this was regarded as a 'retrograde and degenerate novelty' by the outspoken Landseer.

Soft-ground etching, interposing the texture of a piece of paper between a blunt needle and softened varnish, was also used to reproduce chalk and pencil drawings. Turner's friend Wells had published some convincing soft-ground etchings of Gainsborough's drawings between 1803 and 1805. But Turner's intention was never merely to reproduce his own drawings – such an exercise he, like Landseer, would have regarded as flippant. He did use soft-ground, very restrainedly, for Plates 44 and 70, and some unpublished plates of the *Liber*.

Line engraving, with the burin, remained the most exacting technique of all, and the one widely regarded as capable of the most accuracy and expression. The art appears to have struck a dull patch at the end of the eighteenth century, though there were still many excellent engravers. Their skills were perhaps dissipated by the ever-increasing demand for accuracy. The work was almost incredibly slow and painstaking – a large plate could take up to two years to complete. It is surprising that there were not more 'drop-outs' like Blake,* who was an accomplished commercial engraver (in this role he engraved some of Flaxman's classical illustrations). But Blake stands alone in the expressive use of engraving skills. He learnt the art of relief engraving (from his dead brother, in a vision) and was too poor to buy large plates to work on.

The only notable engraver who had worked for Turner at this early stage was James Basire the second – on the Oxford Almanacs. Basire's style was stolid. Turner had to wait until about 1810, when John Pye appeared on the scene, for a line engraver who could interpret him.† Turner later trained and inspired a notable school of line engraving on copper, bringing the art to a final crescendo before steel and wood took over. But this is another story.

Lithography was known (as 'stone-etching') but was believed, in 1806, to be capable of only slight effects. Landseer sums it up inimitably: 'I must remark to you, that it is not the painter's *sketches*, that it is most desirable to multiply, but his *finished performances*.' None of Turner's work was lithographed until 1823, and very little after that.

Etching was the one engraving method that could be practised by a self-respecting artist – the Dutch landscapists having set a precedent. But painter-etchers were few around the turn of the eighteenth to nineteenth century. No

*Some later engravers did become known as artists in their own right. Samuel Middiman, who specialised in the etching stage of line engraving, was one of these, and Luke Clennel, Stothard's engraver (and occasionally Turner's) became known as a watercolourist. Robert Brandard, one of Turner's steel engravers, exhibited oil paintings at the RA. William Radclyffe, the Birmingham engraver, taught his pupils and assistants to draw every day, and to go sketching. Of Turner's regular engravers, Charles Heath and Robert Willmore became ARAs, for engraving.

†On seeing the proofs of *Pope's Villa*, published in 1811, Pye, the engraver of this plate, reported that Turner said: 'Had I known that there was a man who could do that [bring out the lights], I would have had it done before.'

particular value seems to have been put upon autographic reproduction. There was some snobbery, perhaps, about the all-too-necessary business of engraving, and a healthy distrust of facile effects that might be gained from the use of indirect media – see Landseer's remarks above. The academic painters were very serious – even watercolour was regarded with suspicion, and watercolour drawings (not even called paintings) were hung in the darkest corners of the RA.

Rembrandt's etchings were admired by Turner – and admired to the point of slavish imitation by his younger contemporary, Andrew Geddes. Etchings of the more accepted landscape painters such as Ruisdael and Cuyp were known, and indeed the work of John Crome in the early 1800s follows the Dutchmen closely. However, a finely hatched etching manner would not have served Turner in interpreting his own work for *Liber Studiorum*. It would have been too distinctive, and he would have wasted much time on the intricacies of autographic texture, when what he was after was breadth of tone against tone, mass against space. He wanted a substitute for painting itself.

In choosing to etch the line-work of his designs himself, Turner was influenced by purely practical considerations. Still, he was original in planning at this time to exploit engraving for his artistic ends, and was obviously unaffected by current Academy snobbism. Wells, as an engraver and the first president of the breakaway Society of Painters in Watercolour, would clearly have supported him in this.

Engraving *Liber Studiorum*

Turner's first biographer, John Burnet (1852), tells us that the young Turner assisted John Raphael Smith in colouring mezzotints. We can neither corroborate nor disprove this; but Burnet, though he was himself an engraver, was a bad writer (he was a bad engraver) and almost in Thornbury's league for journalistic inaccuracy. There is certainly no hint of an influence from Smith in Turner's early work, unless we take the early self-portrait of 1798 – most of Smith's work was after Reynolds – or the somewhat over-smooth handling of his first exhibited oil painting, *Fishermen at Sea* (1796), as showing an indirect influence. It must be admitted that when Turner first did his own mezzotinting, in 'Junction of the Severn and the Wye' (Plate 28 of the *Liber*), he showed an unexpected aptitude and a tendency to smoothness of gradation that could both have been learnt from Smith, ten years before, although his tones had nothing of J. R. Smith's peculiar density. And on balance, we should perhaps accept Burnet's story as very likely: he would, I feel, be accurate about the recent history of his own trade at least.

The boy Turner certainly lived in the thick of the print business. There were at least two engravers at work in Maiden Lane where he lived behind his father's hairdressing shop. In the area of Covent Garden generally there were at various dates Charles Grignion, History Engraver; Adam Smith, Anatomy and Flower Engraver; Antony Vere, Seal Engraver (in Maiden Lane); Joseph Wood, Landscape Engraver, 'also Remarkable for Engraving Horses'; Woodfield, at the Sign of the Gold Frame, in Maiden Lane. The engravers Darley, Jaubert, Firmin, Blackbeard, Suffield, Scott and others were in the Strand at roughly the same period, as well as numerous painters of all sorts, drawing masters and printsellers. Ackerman's Repository, in the Strand, was opened in 1795. J. R. Smith's 'print publishing business' was in King Street, Covent Garden.

But the Redgrave brothers wrote: 'His birthplace, and the scenes among which Turner passed his childhood, may be thought not to be best fitted to form a landscape painter, or to fill his youthful mind with images of beauty.' Ruskin ('Enchanted oranges gleam in Covent Gardens of the Hesperides') pointed to the drabness of the artist's early surroundings, suggesting that it was responsible for his later celestial purity of colour and his idealisation of Venice (the London Thames transmuted). Perhaps Turner's feelings for landscapes were developed elsewhere, at Brentford, where he spent some apparently formative years from 1785. But both the authorities quoted seem to have forgotten what a forcing-house the district of Covent Garden must have been for a boy with artistic curiosity and leanings.

Turner was certainly familiar with all forms of engraving: just as important, he knew engravers. In setting out upon his own publishing venture he was in a position to choose the method, and the manner, that suited him.

Aquatint he took seriously. He had an excellent precedent in the twenty *Views in Paris* which had been published by John Girtin shortly after his brother's death in 1802. Thomas Girtin had made large pencil drawings in Paris, and, back in London, in the last stages of his illness, had translated these on to the plates in soft-ground etching – with, it may be said, perfect skill and all the appearance of spontaneity. Other artists known to Turner had published sets of 'Views', of course, but Girtin's were outstanding in both conception and execution. A very competent engraver, F. C. Lewis, had added the aquatint tones, usually following proofs 'touched' by the artist.

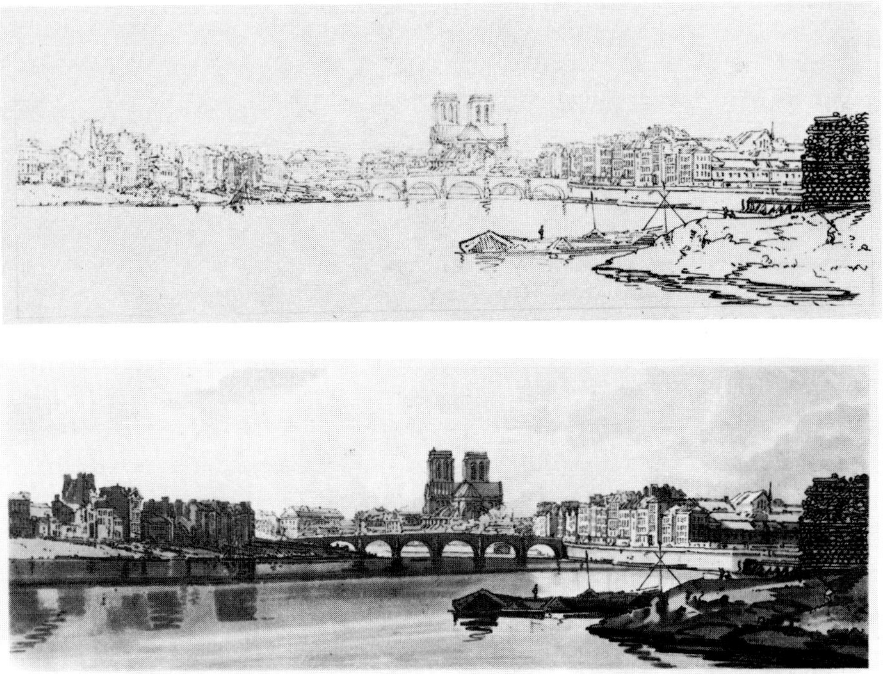

Pont de la Tournelle & Notre Dame from Girtin's *Views in Paris*. Aquatint: Lewis

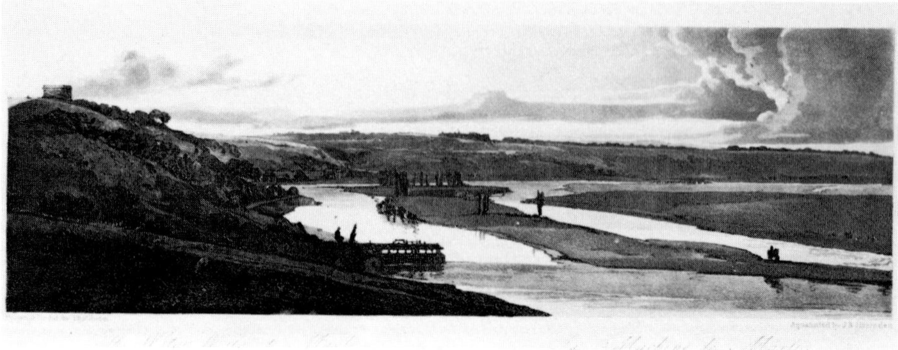

From Girtin's *Views in Paris: Water Works at Marli.* Aquatinted by J. B. Harraden

Turner corresponded with John Girtin about an etching, but the date of the letter is not known and there is not enough evidence to connect it with the *Liber*. In 1806 or 1807 Turner sent Lewis an etched plate for a first trial. This was 'Bridge and Goats', later issued as Plate 43, the aquatint being progressively submerged under mezzotint as the plate was completed. A letter from Turner which must have been written in 1807, because he was at Hammersmith and did not move there until that year, shows that he asked Lewis to proceed with a further plate 'without an etching' – Turner would etch the lines after the aquatint. Lewis, who was busy at the time engraving the Royal Collection (including many Claude drawings) asked for 8 guineas instead of 5 as agreed for the first, already etched, plate. Turner refused this.

Lewis was getting from 15 to 40 guineas for the royal Claudes, so he was understandably impatient with Turner, whose etchings did not even follow his own originals. But he wrote much later, in 1850, that he regretted this: 'he 'ought not to have considered the price of the plates of any object compared to the fame for such fine works'.

We may wonder if they would have got very far with the aquatinted plates, and whether Turner was making the price an excuse for not continuing – as I suggest he may have done with Charles Turner at a later stage in the publication. He seems to have become prejudiced against the use of aquatint except for the light tones of his skies. When, in *Dunstanborough Castle* (Plate 14), the engraver carried the aquatint a little further – Finberg says, to avoid a jump in 'colour' – Turner rebuked him, scribbling in the margin of the proof, 'Sir, – You have done in aquatint all the Castle down to the rocks. Did I ever ask for such an indulgence?'

By the time Lewis was dismissed Turner had already issued Part 1 of the *Liber*, all in mezzotint by his old classmate of the Academy Schools, Charles Turner. Charles had produced, during 1806, a large mezzotint of J.M.W.'s *Shipwreck*, and published it at his own expense (1 January 1807), apparently very successfully. Turner certainly must have been influenced by this venture in his planning for *Liber Studiorum*. The *Shipwreck No. 1* sketchbook (LXXXVII) is endorsed on the cover in Turner's hand, 'Subscriber's List', and includes about a hundred names of those who might be interested in the *Liber* publication.

Charles Turner was not the ideal engraver for Turner. Though very competent, his work lacks a certain delicacy of touch. But the partnership continued, and Charles for a time took a large part of the responsibility for the publication. Turner was rather slow in getting Part 2 ready. This is not surprising when we note that he had fifteen oil paintings on show in 1808 and twenty in 1809, including the works exhibited in his own gallery. He put the 'publication and management' of the *Liber* in the hands of his friend the engraver. Charles also was slow – 'the plates not done – not advertised, in short everything has conspired against the work', complained Turner to him, early in 1808.

Part 3 came out in June of that year and Part 4 in the following March, completing twenty plates engraved by Charles Turner. Then Charles asked for an extra 2 guineas a plate. As he wrote in 1852: 'A misunderstanding was the consquence, which lasted nineteen years' – he was out of favour, in the middle of his work on Part 5. But the quarrel cannot have lasted as long as he says, for he engraved *Norham Castle* (Plate 57), published in 1816, and other later plates.

In the further progress of the work Turner employed altogether a dozen different engravers, dividing each part between three or four men.

He etched most of the plates himself, working on a ground prepared for him by the engraver with a tracing of the main lines of his original drawing. After he had drawn as many lines as he thought necessary on the wax, he returned the plate for biting in, probably indicating where the plate was to be bitten more than once, for more emphatic lines. Then several proofs of the etching were taken – a dozen or more – though only one or two were needed. Thus Turner gave to the world a unique series of autograph etchings, which vary from 'rare' to 'very rare' in the salerooms. They are perhaps overvalued, for they are only skeletons of the works. The impressions are usually on Whatman paper, as distinct from the softer Auvergne which was used for the printing except when supplies ran out because of the war with France.

In some cases an etching proof was used by Turner to wash in sepia tones for the engraver's guidance, but usually the drawn cartoon was sufficient guide. He usually kept several proofs of the etchings. No less than twenty-two proofs of the *Greenwich* etching (Plate 26) survived to be sold after his death. He had ordered fifty prints: did he intend to colour them? He had not been above tinting some late prints of the *Shipwreck*.

Of one out of seventy-eight finished plates, number 55, *Entrance of Calais Harbour*, no etched state is known, and of two where soft-ground etching was used (Plates 44 and 70) only one or two impressions survive – sadly, for they are among the most attractive. Four plates were etched not by Turner but (probably all) by Dawe; two of these were mezzotinted by Turner over Dawe's line-work. Twelve of the published plates he did entirely on his own – so the inscription informs us. The later, unpublished plates were also all Turner's own work, occasionally in collaboration with Henry Dawe.

In the etchings Turner used an emphatic line (usually, I believe, the result of successive bitings perhaps aided by a heavier, thicker needle) for nearer, darker or more heavily modelled parts of the design. Distant contours and areas of light modelling were bitten very lightly. This gives the best of the etchings their characteristic quality of modulation and aerial perspective – very noticeably absent in the etchings by other hands, such as *Mill near the Grand Chartreuse* (Plate 54) or *The Source of the Arveron* (Plate 60). The heaviest etched lines often hardly remain visible under the subsequent dark mezzotint, but are still attractively tactile in relief: a quality which eludes our half-tone reproduction.

The skies he invariably left blank, even where, as in *Peat Bog* (Plate 45), *Solway Moss* (Plate 52) or *Watercress Gatherers* (Plate 62) the sky is filled with dark, stormy clouds. He sometimes varied his methods by adding bits of mezzotint (Plates 28 and 39). But in the great majority of the etchings the line remains bald and, to me, unsatisfying, and the composition lacking in balance. It is as if one heard the woodwind and percussion parts only of a fine orchestral piece: not exactly a sketchy account, but undoubtedly inadequate. In some of the etchings a multiplicity of detail makes up for the lack of balance and cloaks the nakedness of the line, producing an effect of controlled intricacy such as we know from the early sketchbooks.

Finberg's enthusiasm is difficult to share: Turner's line-work, he says, is '... so free from affectation and self-consciousness, so straightforward, so honest, so fearless and genial, so effortless, so sensitive, yet so thoroughly workmanlike'.

Well, certainly it is workmanlike. Hamerton, writing in 1879, feels something similar, though he is careful, as a practical etcher himself, to point out that Turner had over-simplified his task, and was not much of an etcher; but, he says, 'The work with the etching needle . . . is full of masculine economy and strength.'

Frank Short, RA, paid Turner the greatest compliment by copying many of his etchings and engravings. In a lecture in 1924 he said: 'These "preliminary etchings" . . . are the finest things in the world in landscape drawing.' And, 'I consider this kind of etching more difficult than any other [he should have known], and it is owing to Turner's life-long practice of drawing with a hard pencil point, his absolute knowledge of all landscape form, his wonderful power in composition in the relation of line to line, and his freedom in etching his own drawings – apart from the grandeur of the compositions as a whole – that these preliminary etchings convey so much joy and instruction.' In turn, it may be noticed from the sketchbooks, etching began to influence Turner's pencil line around 1815.

In later mezzotints the etching stage was dispensed with. In *Rivers of England* Turner was able to hand over with confidence a finished watercolour to his well-tried team of engravers, and in the 'Little Liber' plates, which he obviously scraped himself, there is no hint of the needle.

Before *Liber Studiorum*, mezzotint had not been used for original landscape work. Turner worked out his own method. He kept control, while employing, in all, fourteen different engravers; and the method worked, even allowed a certain amount of development. It was not perfect, and I believe that the later, unpublished plates show that the line-work had been an embarrassment in exploiting the true expressiveness of the medium.

The engraved plates wore out quickly in the press. In 1852, when there was some perplexity at the large number – 5,020 – of unsold prints found amongst Turner's belongings, Pye, Charles Turner, Lahee and Lupton signed a statement; to quote Lahee: 'Having printed the plates of the Liber Studiorum I beg to say they were copper and produced on the average from twenty to thirty proofs of a fine class.' Pye thought Turner dishonest in passing off the renovated plates as first states. To Turner, of course, they were his work and he was satisfied with them. In fact he usually made some small mark in the margin, or a dot in one of the letters, so that he should know his children if he met them.

This refurbishing process and the trial proofs resulting from it have led to the identifying of as many as five or six, normally three or four, but in one case

Dunstanborough Castle from his 'North of England' Sketchbook, XXXIV, of 1797

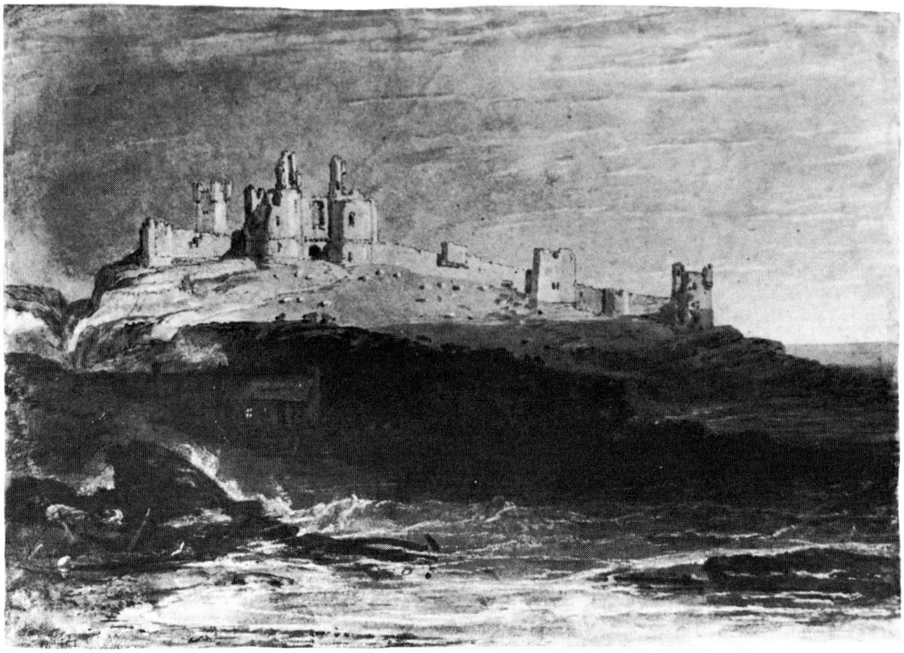

Drawing about 1806, for *Liber Studiorum*, CXVI Q. This and the sketch above are about the same size as the engraving, $10\frac{1}{2}$ inches (27 cm) wide

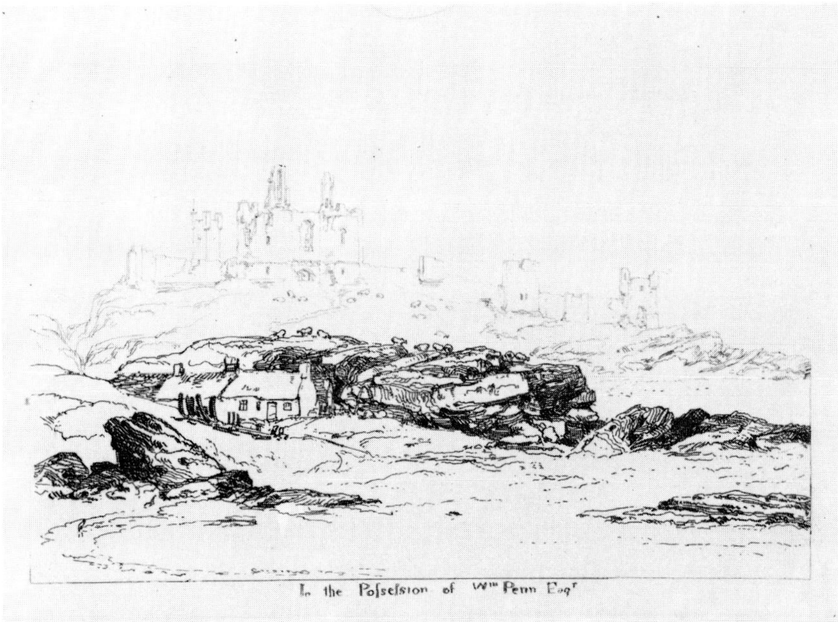

Turner's etching. Below, enlarged detail from the published plate, with aquatint sky and mezzotint over the etched lines. See Plate 14

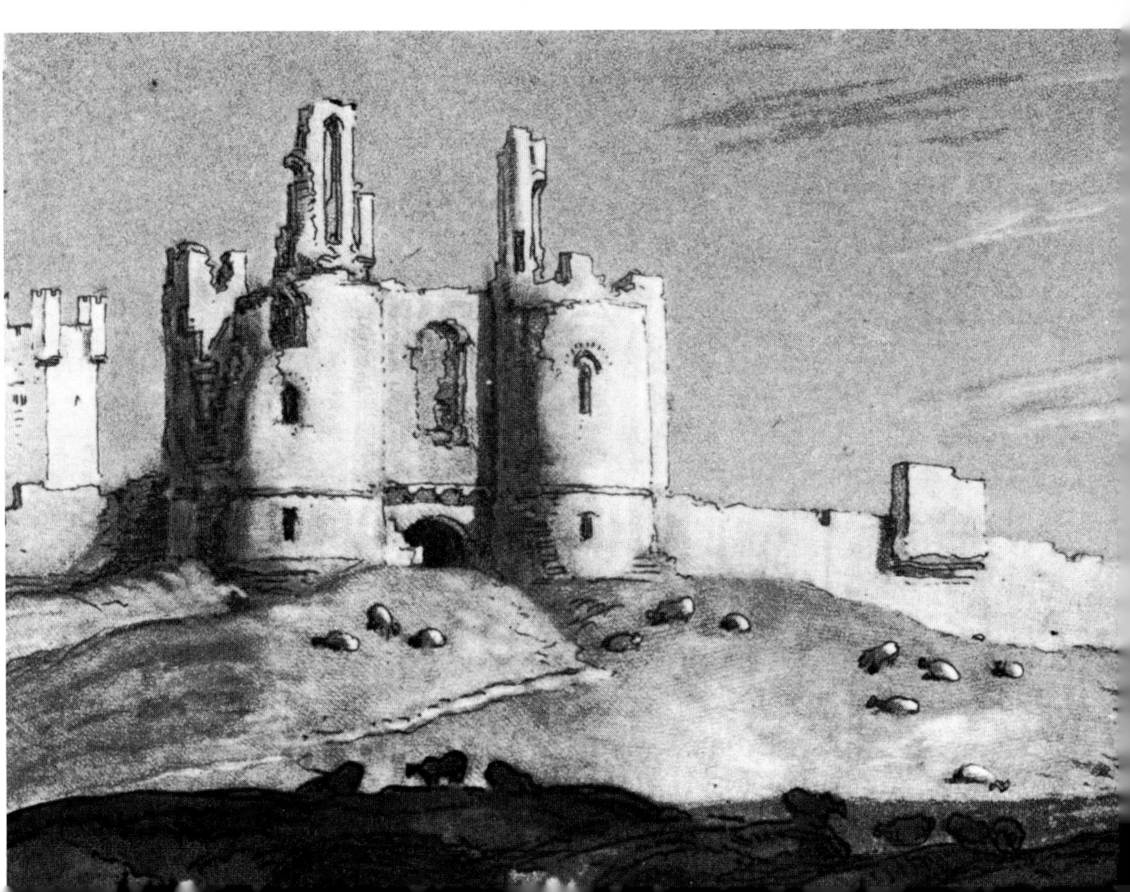

(Plate 44) seven different states. Third, fourth and even fifth states are often described by Finberg as 'still fine', or 'fine in early impressions'. Readers interested in identifying a particular state are referred to Finberg's *History of Turner's Liber Studiorum*. Much as I appreciate the velvety (unreproduceable) tones of the finest impressions, I think that those from the worn plates often reveal more of the formal design. And you need an eagle's eye to spot some of the differences so important to collectors.

Before the published versions we find as many as eight different 'engraver's proofs' showing usually minor corrections to detail, balance and tone. Turner and his engravers finished their work by scraping extra highlights, polishing minor gradations, sharpening detail by the use of dry-point, clarifying sunrays, and so on. It often occurs that the flatter, softer effect of an earlier trial or 'engraver's proof', before all this 'making out' was done, is more satisfactory, at least to my eyes. I have included illustrations of some of these trial proofs where I feel they show something of the artist's intention before his work was polished for public consumption. Admirers of Turner will be aware of this schism. Of course, part of the purpose of the finishing touches was to offset the dulling of the plate as it wore under the press.

All the plates following are first published states unless otherwise described.

The published plates

There is no indication in Turner's notebooks that he planned each part of his *Liber* to demonstrate a particular theme. The use here of the expression 'unifying theme' is not intended to imply that Turner chose themes and designed his plates to illustrate them. But I think the themes are there and were part and parcel of his whole approach to his work at this period of his life. In some cases, perhaps, he was guided by a definite theme; in others, the theme results from his putting together certain subjects – it 'emerges'. No-one can collate fourteen batches of five pictures each without considering what they have in common, what their total effect is, how they contrast, and so on.

Turner was concerned first of all to put one subject from five of his six categories (Pastoral, Marine, etc.) in each set. This ensured a reasonable range of material for each published part. His choice of alternatives was always limited and must have been governed at times by delays and accidents. His list of parts and subjects planned in (about) 1809 (see the '*Liber* Notes 2' sketchbook, CLIVa) would not have resulted in the same range of 'themes' that I have discovered.

It is only a way of looking at the material. Anyone may say that I am wrong in perceiving this or that theme, or they may see a different one. This does not matter. It is sufficient that we look again at the plates in their published sequence and learn what we may. I believe that it is no more true to say that Turner's *Liber Studiorum* was intended merely to show off his skill in different categories of landscape than it is to claim that Bach's forty-eight preludes and fugues were merely to demonstrate the usefulness of equal temperament.

But we should not expect to find a pedagogic master-plan. It was never a course in composition. Like all Turner's series (including his life's work as a whole), it was bound to be open-ended, never finished, because nature and experience themselves are never complete.

Rawlinson concludes the introduction to his catalogue (1878 and 1906) with a long quotation from Ruskin, which he says he cannot agree with – but it is 'so characteristic'. I cannot agree with it either, but it deserves repetition. It is from the end of Volume V of *Modern Painters* (1860). 'Raglan' is Plate 58.

Take up the Liber Studiorum, and observe how this feeling of decay and humiliation gives solemnity to all its simplest subjects; even to his view of daily labour. I have marked its tendency in examining the design of the 'Mill and Lock', but observe its continuance through the book. There is no exultation in thriving city or mart, or in happy rural toil, or harvest gathering. Only the grinding at the mill, and patient striving with hard conditions of life. Observe the two disordered and poor farmyards, cart, and ploughshare, and harrow rotting away; note the pastoral by the brook side, with its neglected stream, and haggard trees, and bridge with the broken rail; and decrepit children – fever struck – one sitting stupidly by the stagnant stream, the other in rags, and with an old man's hat on, and lame, leaning on a stick. Then the 'Hedging and Ditching', with its bleak sky and blighted trees, hacked, and bitten, and starved by the clay soil into something between trees and firewood; its meanly-faced, sickly labourers, like the willow trunk they hew; and the slatternly peasant-woman, with worn cloak and battered bonnet – an English Dryad. Then the Water-Mill, beyond the fallen steps, overgrown with the thistle: itself a ruin, mud-built at first, now propped on both sides; the planks torn from its cattle shed; a feeble beam splintered at the end, set against the dwelling-house from the ruined pier of the watercourse; the old mill-stone – useless for many a day – half buried in slime, at the bottom of the wall; the listless children, listless dog, and the poor gleaner bringing her single sheaf to be ground. Then the 'Peat Bog', with its cold, dark rain, and dangerous labour. And last the chief, the mill in the valley of the Chartreuse. Another than Turner would have painted the convent, but he had no sympathy with the hope, no mercy for the indolence, of the monk. He painted the mill in the valley. Precipice overhanging it, and wilderness of dark forest round; blind rage and strength of mountain torrent rolled beneath it, – calm sunset above, but fading from the glen, leaving it to its roar of passionate waters and sighing of pine-branches in the night.

Such is his view of human labour. Of human pride, see what he records. Morpeth Tower, roofless and black; gate of old Winchelsea wall, the flock of sheep driven round it, not through it; and Rievaulx choir, and Kirkstall crypt; and Dunstanborough, wan above the sea; and Chepstow, with arrowy light through traceried windows; and Lindisfarne, with failing height of wasted shaft and wall; and last and sweetest, Raglan, in utter solitude, amidst the wild wood of its own pleasance; the towers rounded with ivy, and the forest roots choked with undergrowth, and the brook languid amidst lilies and sedges. Legends of gray knights and enchanted ladies keeping the woodman's children away at the sunset.

These are his types of human pride. Of human love: Procris, dying by the arrow; Hesperie, by the viper's fang; and Rizpah, more than dead, beside her children.

Such are the lessons of the Liber Studiorum. Silent always with a bitter silence, disdaining to tell his meaning, when he saw there was no ear to receive it, Turner only indicated his purpose by slight words of contemptuous anger, when he heard of any one's trying to obtain this or the other separate subject as more beautiful than the rest. 'What is the use of them,' he said, 'but together?' The meaning of the entire book was symbolized in the frontispiece, which he engraved with his own hand: Tyre at Sunset, with the Rape of Europa, indicating the symbolism of the decay of Europe by that of Tyre, its beauty passing away into terror and judgement (Europa being the mother of Minos and Rhadamanthus).

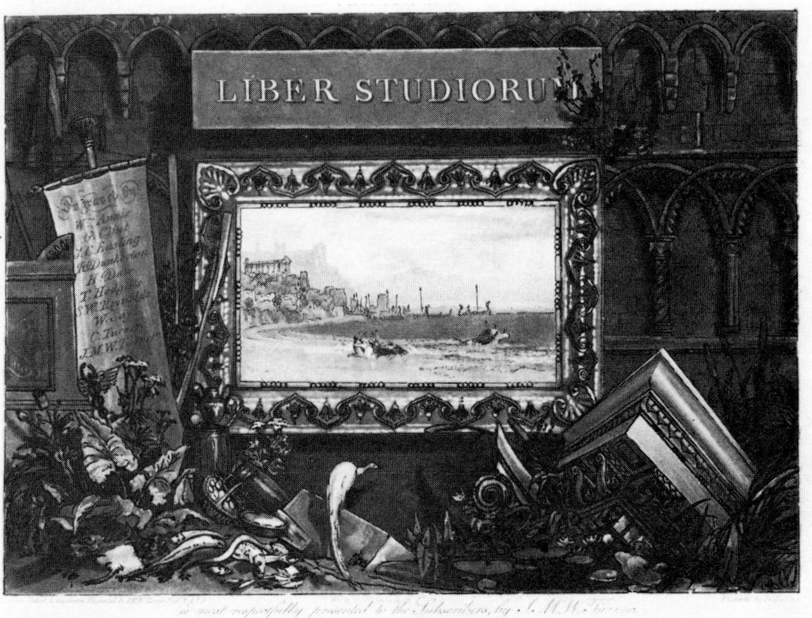

The 'Frontispiece' or title plate issued to subscribers with Part 10. It is numbered as Plate 1 in the catalogues

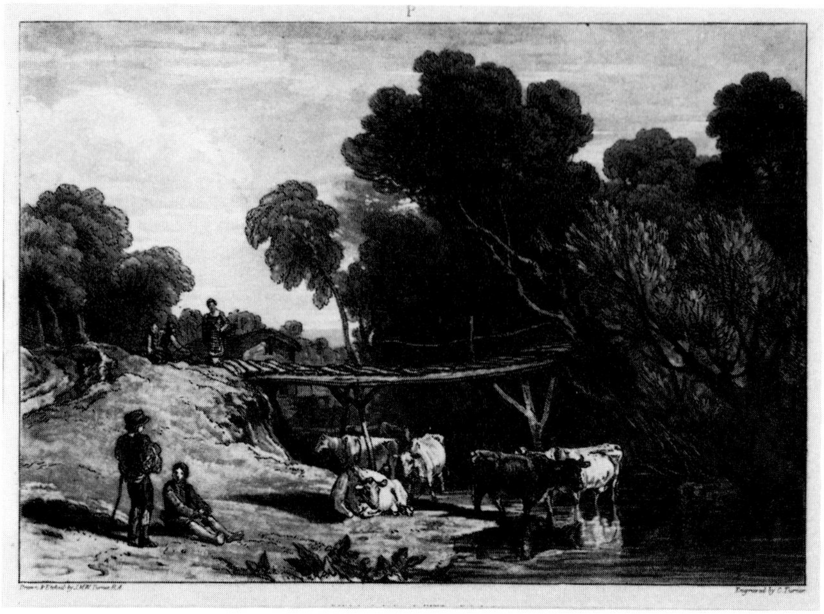

Plate 2 (P) 'Bridge and Cows'

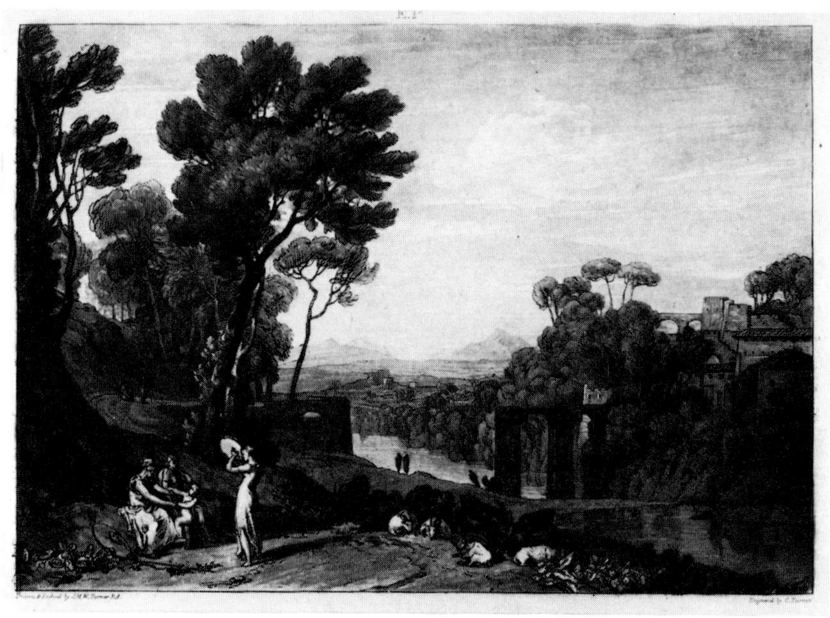

Plate 3 (EP) 'Woman with Tambourine'

PART **I** 11 June 1807

Only connect . . .

For his first essay Turner takes a simple, yet at the same time highly symbolic, theme: the bridge. Though it is a poetic and even metaphysical symbol, the idea of a bridge is, of course, in no way fundamental to landscape composition. At the conversational level it is a cliché: as an emblem for Turner's ambition in his 'Book of Studies' it is fine. He does not labour the point, merely using a bridge as a unifying theme for the first set of plates. We may see the set as a prelude or preliminary flourish. The point he is making, surely, is the importance of the *subject.*

He loved arches. An arched bridge is very commonly a focal point in his paintings, and he drew arches over and over again in his sketches. Rainbows equally delighted and obsessed him, and he often drew the setting sun as a bridge – perhaps into another world. But the bridges here are noticeably un-arched and impermanent. The emphasis is on the act of crossing. Stone arches, as Turner drew them, have a timeless sculptural quality, and they are as much a way through for the river as a way over for the people; or they fly across ravines, as in Plate 19, or are looped together across the distances of many expansive river scenes.

In the first plate of the *Liber* the bridge is a simple meeting of country ways. It leads rather mysteriously into the little wood, but the pull of the light invites us to stay on the warm bank, where everything seems to have paused for the whole of a summer afternoon. Turner gave the plate no title, just headed it with the letter P, for Pastoral.

The second composition, 'Woman with Tambourine', was referred to by Turner as his 'EP Bridge', and as 'Claude EP'. Ruskin said that it owed 'the principal part of its imbecilities to Claude', which is one way of putting it. We stand at a greater distance. Can we mistake the symbolism of the broken span and missing pier as that link, which Turner means to repair in his works, between the classical background and the modern context?

'Scene on the French Coast', or 'Flint Castle' – the plate again has no title – features a more tenuous bridge, formed by a cart and horses. It is a bridge

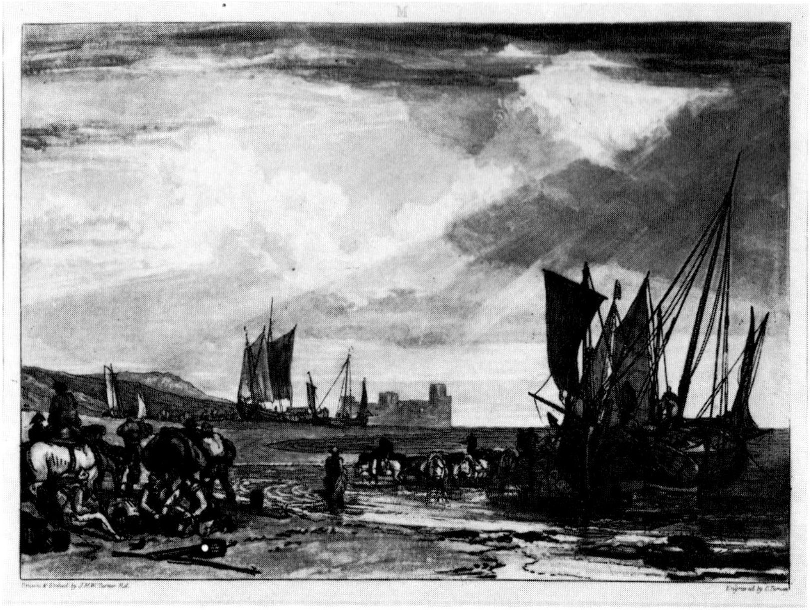

Plate 4 (M) 'Scene on the French Coast', or 'Flint Castle'

between sea and land, equally the proper subjects of the landscapist. With a tremendous accretion of radiating lines from the top right, and a remarkable huddle of men and horses at the bottom left, Turner also reminds us of the animal and the celestial elements. While the drawing for the plate is relatively empty and neutral, it seems that the inspiration of Claude, as much as in the previous plate, has carried the engraving to a much greater intensity of effect.

In *Basle** the bridge is picturesque and a fundamental unit of the composition – as it is of the life of the town. By its catching the sunlight (and, with its minute procession, our interest) and setting back the distance, it balances, though relatively weightless, the whole mass of buildings in the right half of the picture.

Jason, from a favourite painting of Turner's but not of anyone else, is built up of natural bridges, though they are not essential to the theme. Jason is about to end the life of the magic serpent with his sword, securing the golden fleece it had guarded until Medea, employing superior magic, had put it to sleep. Jason will also win the fratricidal Medea: perhaps he thinks he is crossing his last bridge. Turner, with his ambitions, and a better chance of the golden fleece than most of

*Italics are used for Turner's published titles only; others are put in quotes.

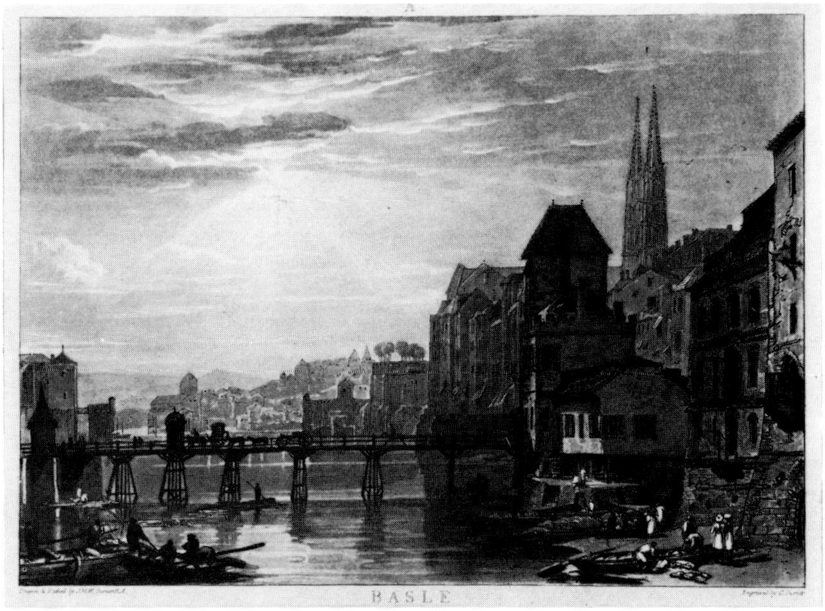

Plate 5 (A) *Basle*

us, would surely have identified with Jason. If he had wanted another, more obvious, bridge there are plenty of Historical ones he could have chosen.

Ruskin thought there was 'something of the nineteenth century about his [Jason's] legs'. But he wrote a fine, long passage about the plate (*Modern Painters*, 1846, vol. 2, p. 166). He notes: 'The trunks of the trees on the right, all cloven into yawning and writhing heads and bodies, and alive with dragon energy . . .' And perhaps this is the bridge we must make in our minds; it is a necessary part of the appreciation of landscape art.

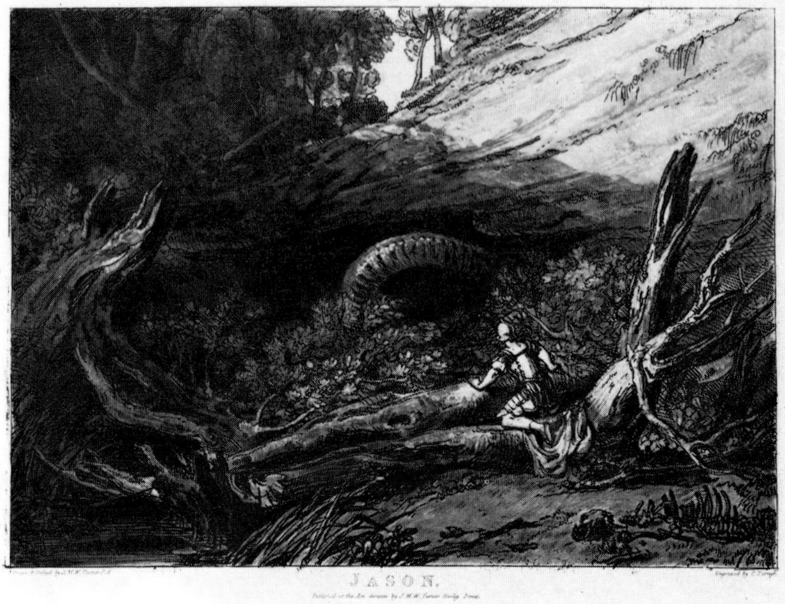

Plate 6 (H) *Jason*

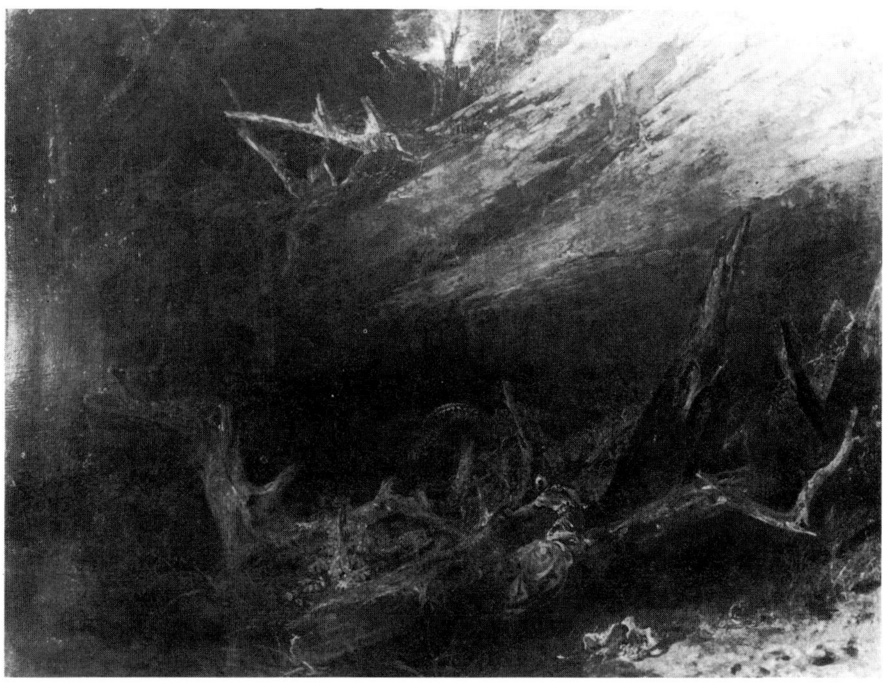

The oil painting, 3 feet by 4 feet (91 × 122 cm), first exhibited in 1802. Tate Gallery

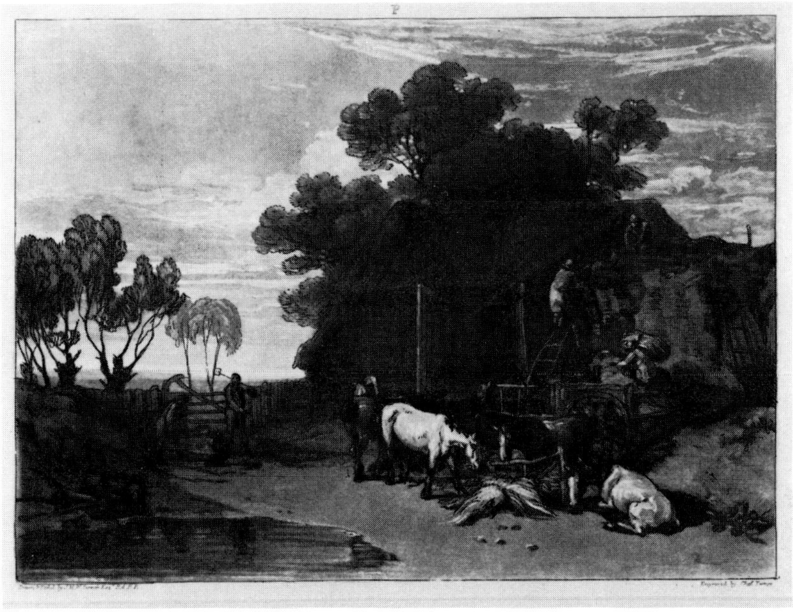

Plate 7 (P) 'The Straw Yard'

PART 2 20 February 1808

'White when it shines'

An autumnal air hangs in the plates of this set. It is possible that Turner intended it to be published late in 1807, but was delayed – he went off to Portsmouth to draw HMS *Victory*, and lingered in Sussex on the way back, observing ploughmen and horses, noting in his sketchbook, 'Hind Head; Water Mill; Pigg's sty; St Catherine's Hill'. In the meantime he handed over the business of publication to his engraver and friend, Charles Turner.

'The Straw Yard' had no title, but Turner gave us the key to this part in his name for this plate – 'The White Horse'. The use of white in landscape, and in painting generally, was a controversial subject. Turner and some young followers were called, derogatorily, 'the white painters'. John Gage (*Colour in Turner*, 1969, p. 97), says that Girtin's *The White House at Chelsea* 'was for Turner possibly the most influential colour-composition in the work of a contemporary'. Certainly he wrote 'Tom Girtin' on many sketches throughout his life and long after Girtin's death. Turner, I believe, missed Girtin – for who else of his contemporaries could he have really respected? His only recorded, and probably apocryphal, comment was the wry and hardly sincere: 'If Tom Girtin had lived, I should have starved.' The relationship between the young Turner and Girtin is always debatable: born in the same year, working together at Dr Monro's copies; following each other, apparently, on sketching tours and picking the same subjects as if in rivalry; Girtin, defiantly amateur, with his circle of sketching companions; Turner, the plodding Academy student 'alone and on horseback'. Girtin died when aged 27, and it is not too extravagant to conceive this chapter of the *Liber* as Turner's monument to him – who, it may be remembered, had beaten him to the post in producing etchings of his own watercolours.

Through Reynolds, whose last lectures he probably attended, Turner was familiar with Du Fresnoy's theories on painting, and later painted a *Watteau Study by Fresnoy's Rules* (1831 – 'all in a mere sketch and apparently produced without effort', wrote a critic). For the legend to this picture Turner quoted from the following translation from Du Fresnoy, published in 1783:

> White when it shines with sustain'd luster clear
> May bear an object back or bring it near.
> Aided by black, it to the front aspires;
> That aid withdrawn, it distantly retires;
> But black unmix'd of darkest midnight hue,
> Still calls each object nearer to the view.

What this, if true, has got to do with Watteau, I don't know. While it must be admitted that in these monochrome plates the white could not have the value it would have in relation to colour, it was important enough to occupy at least part of his attention.

The second, Elevated Pastoral plate (Plate 8) employs a white cow instead of a horse. In the 'MS' (Mountainous) *Mt St Gothard* it is the Alpine peaks that provide the white, now remote instead of close. 'Make the lights pure white', wrote Turner to the engraver. This distant white is echoed by the light at the end of the tunnel.

The ships in 'Ships in a Breeze' have, some of them, white sails, and the water

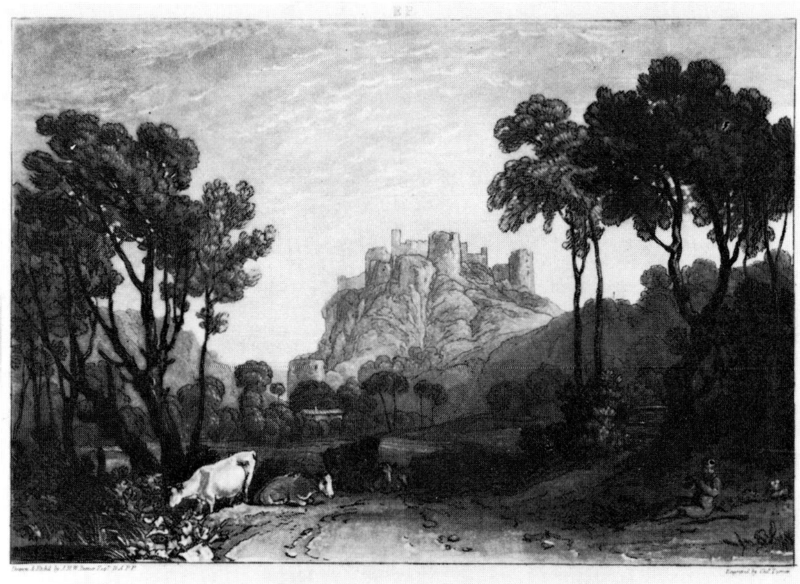

Plate 8 (EP) 'Castle above Meadows'. 3rd published state

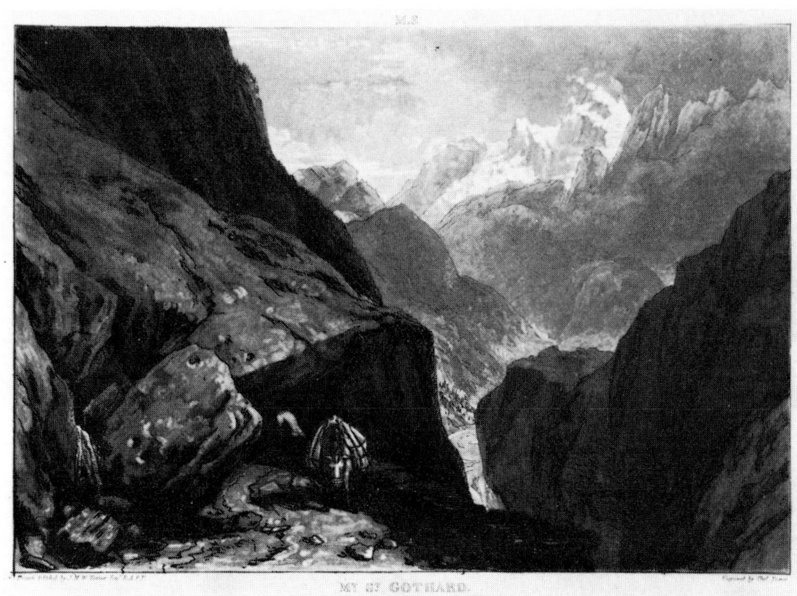

Plate 9 (MS) *Mt St Gothard.*

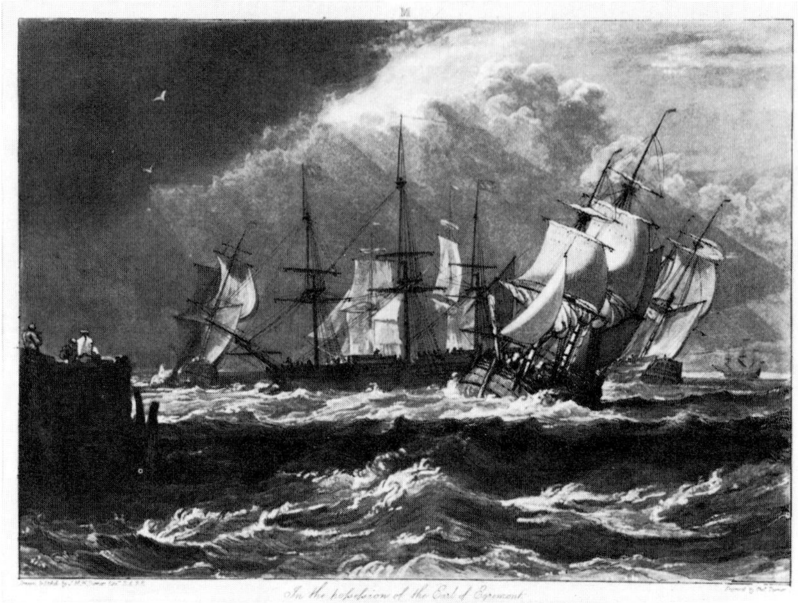

Plate 10 (M) 'Ships in a Breeze'

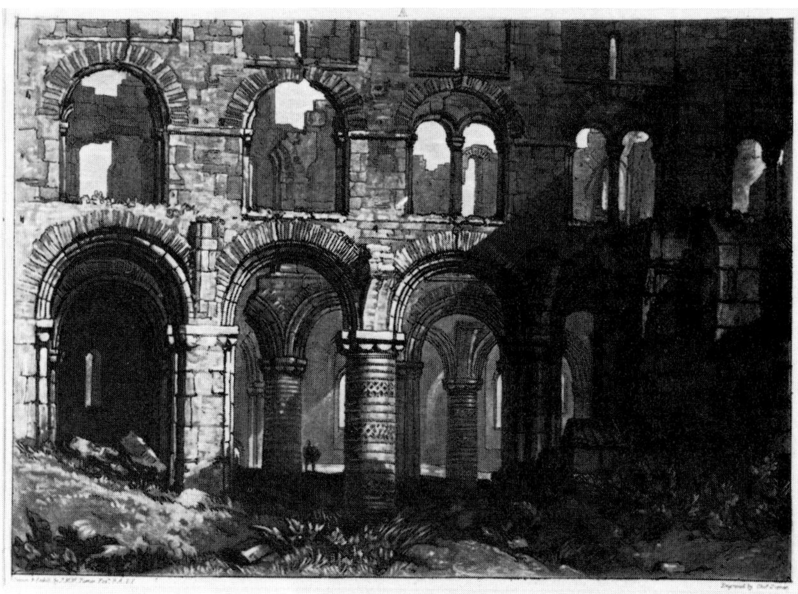

Plate 11 (A) *Holy Island Cathedral*

is broken into white-crested waves. White is used in a different way in *Holy Island Cathedral* as patches of white sky, negative rather than positive.

But a second theme is almost as important: patterns of void and solid. They are vigorously exploited throughout the set, from, in the farmyard, every sort of frame and lattice, through the cave, crevasse and ravine of *Mt St Gothard* and the complex orrery of the wheeling ships, to the parallel, pierced planes of *Holy Island Cathedral*. Only in Turner's 'EP Castle' is sentiment allowed to take precedence over construction, the void and solid reduced to a simple monumentality, a gate and the trees merely echoing the strong patterns of the first plate. Even so, of the sculptured rock on which the castle stands, Rawlinson was able to write, 'the delicate mezzotinting . . . lighting and defining its hollows and buttress-like crags'.

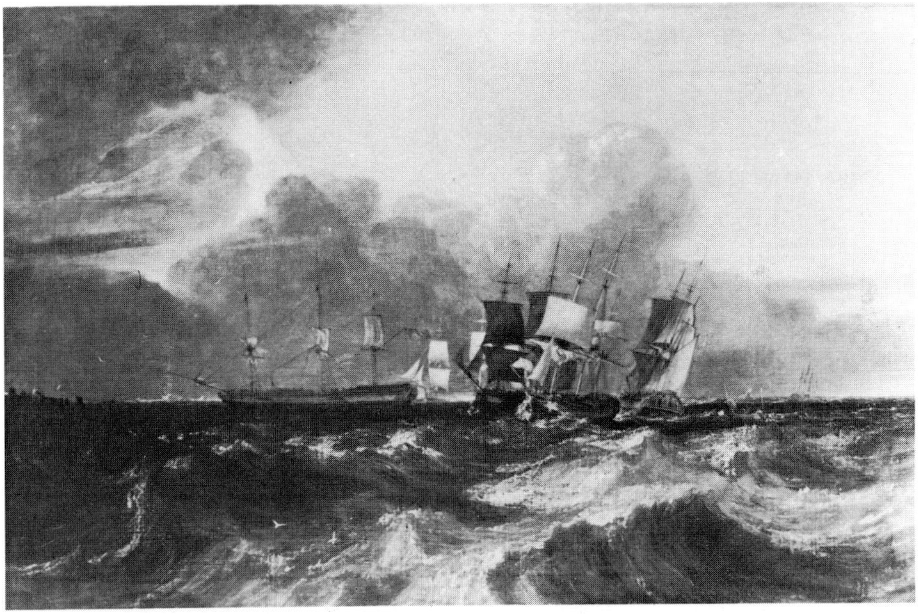

Ships bearing up for Anchorage – the 'Egremont Sea Piece'. Plate 10 of the *Liber* is an adaptation of this picture, which is about 4 × 6 feet (122 × 183 cm), to a mezzotint of approximately 7 × 10 inches (18 × 25 cm).

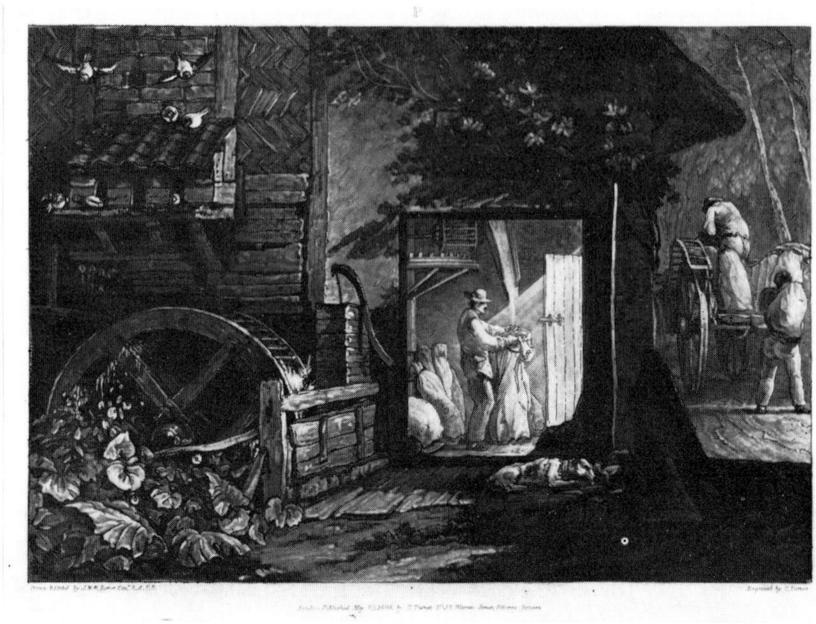

Plate 12 (P) *Pembury Mill, Kent.* Engraver's proof

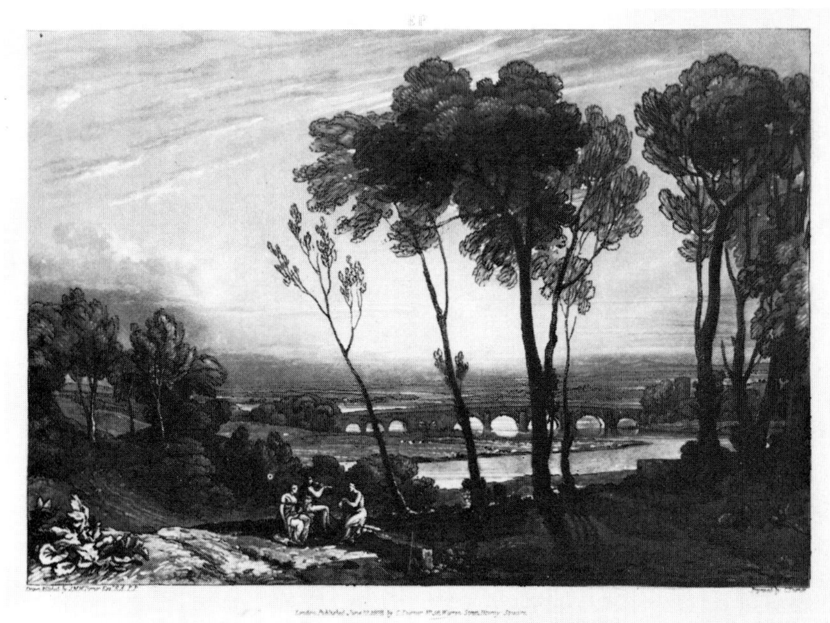

Plate 13 (EP) 'Bridge in Middle Distance'

PART **3** 10 June 1808

'Forms peculiar . . .'

The unifying theme of solid geometry is too obvious to miss: the insistence on cubic and cylindrical compartments, parallel to the picture plane, in *Pembury Mill*; the neat, round and square blocks of *Dunstanborough* (contrasted with 'shapeless' sea and rocks); the pyramids of *The Fifth Plague* under their terrible parallelogram of light. In *Lake of Thun* the basic geometry is less obvious, but the U-shaped valley – half a hollow cylinder – and the boldly stated plane of the lake are the main units of the composition. Hollowness is emphasised by the path of the lightning and a ceiling of heavy cloud. In the foreground the wheels of Pembury Mill appear again, altered only slightly.

In the remaining plate, the Elevated Pastoral 'Bridge in Middle Distance', the geometry is not so striking a theme: it is more assimilated. Turner's name for this plate, 'Walton Bridge', reminds us that it was a favourite subject (see the later

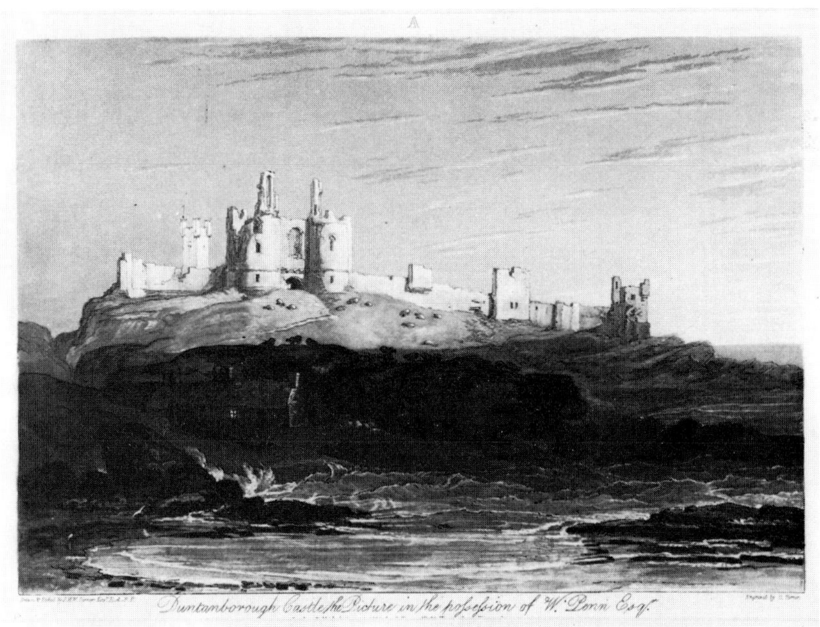

Plate 14 (A) *Dunstanborough Castle*

England and Wales composition where he repeats the pattern of the semi-circular arches in counterpoint and, using their reflections, inversion). In the *Liber* plate the grouping of the three musicians, and their pseudo-classical dress, hint at Poussin, that most obsessively geometrical painter. The triplet is repeated, subtly varied, in the intervals of the tree-trunks and their shadows.

A sub-theme of the set is the use of special lighting effects: the strongly lit interior in *Pembury Mill*, the 'back-lighting' of the 'Bridge', *Dunstanborough*'s pale dawn light over shadow, the storm light of *Lake of Thun*, the dramatic fall of light in *The Fifth Plague*.

Turner became Professor of Perspective at the Royal Academy in December, 1807. Each plate in this third set bears the letters RAPP after his name – 'Drawn and etched by . . .'. In the notes for one of his professorial lectures he adapted some lines from Akenside:

> Such the use of forms
> Peculiar in the realms of Space or Time:
> Such is the throne which Man for truth amid
> The paths of mutability hath built
> Secure, unshaken, still; and whence he views,
> In matter's mouldering structures, the pure forms
> Of Triangle or Circle, Cube or Cone.

A late oil painting, *Landscape with Walton Bridge*, was based on Plate 13. It is in the collection of Henry Morgan, New York.

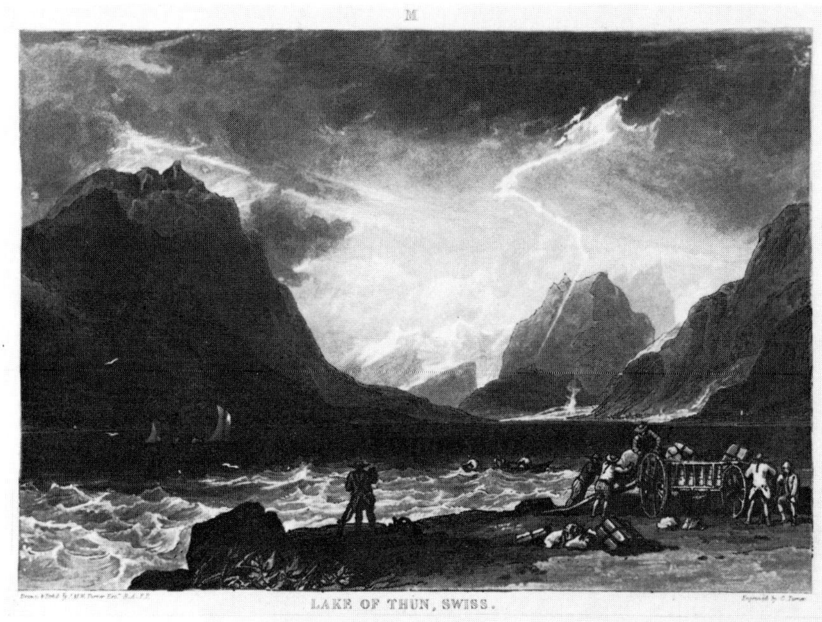

Plate 15 (M) *Lake of Thun, Swiss*

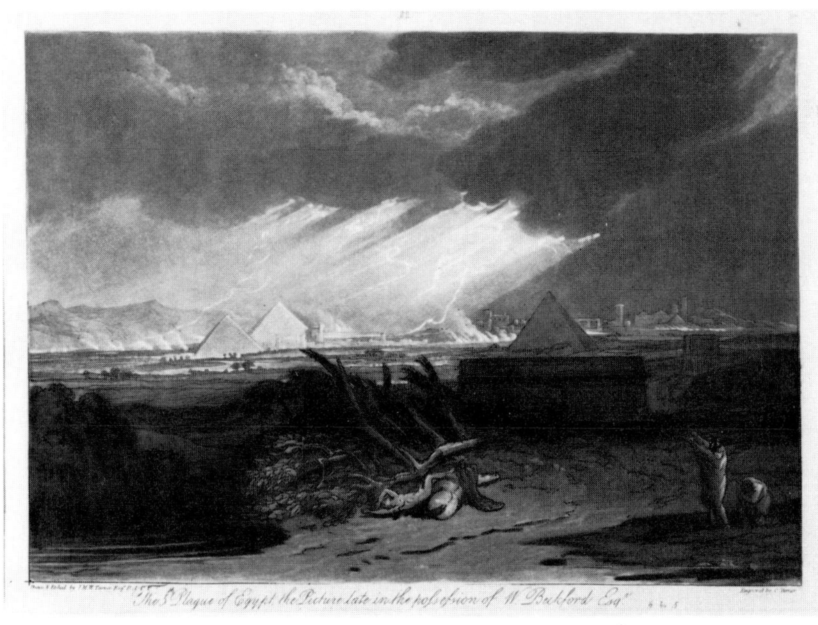

Plate 16 (H) *The 5th Plague of Egypt*

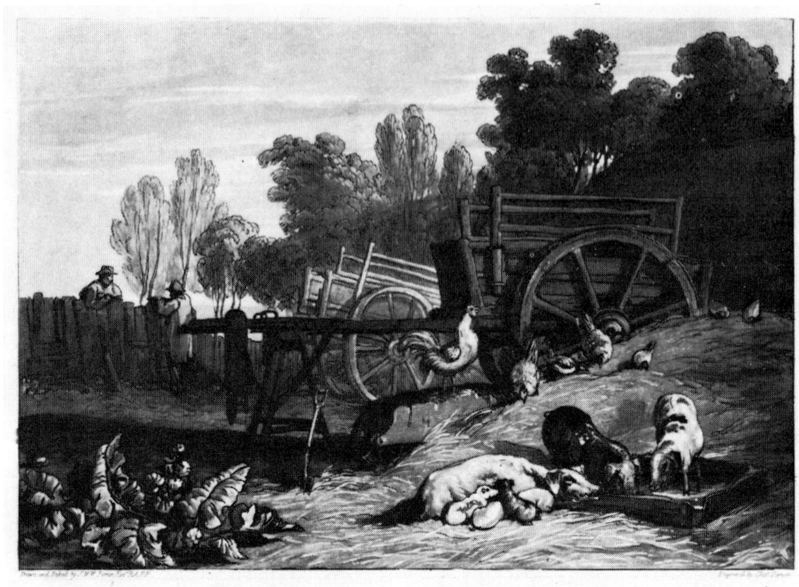

Plate 17 (P) 'Farmyard with a Cock'

PART 4 29 March 1809

Allegories of movement

Having so far established the importance of (1) subject, (2) accent and pattern, and (3) geometry and lighting, Turner now moves on to an equally important, but sometimes neglected, aspect of landscape composition: movement. He starts, perhaps obscurely, but reasonably enough, with the arrested movement of his Pastoral plate. The farmyard is at rest in the evening calm, figures motionless at the fence, trees still; the massive carts are symbols of the theme. Only the animals stir.

In *Drawing of the Clyde* he cleverly augments the force of the waterfall with directional light, bringing unexpected dynamism to an Elevated Pastoral. The highest of the Clyde Falls is 90 feet, so the scale provided by the classical bathing girls may be poetic and not hyperbolic. In the original watercolour they

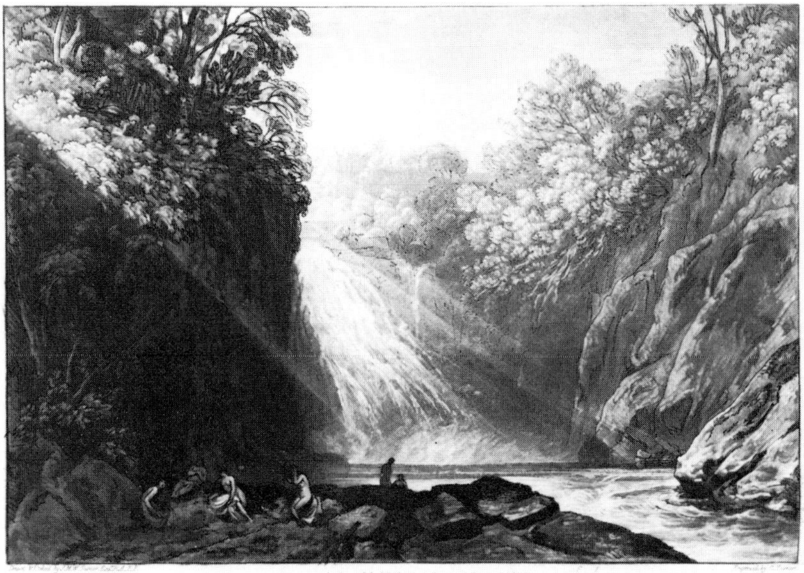

Plate 18 (EP) *Drawing of the Clyde*. 3rd published state

Below, the watercolour, about 30 × 41 inches (76 × 104 cm), exhibited in 1802. Walker Art Gallery, Liverpool

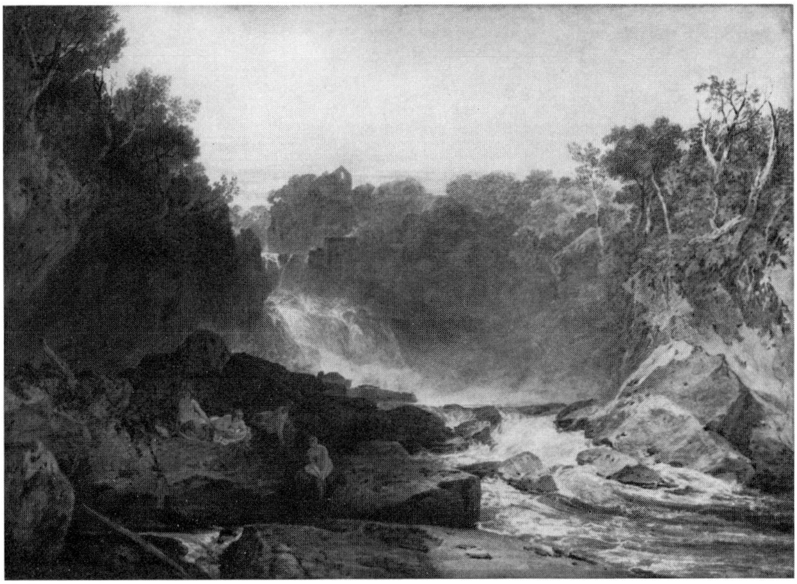

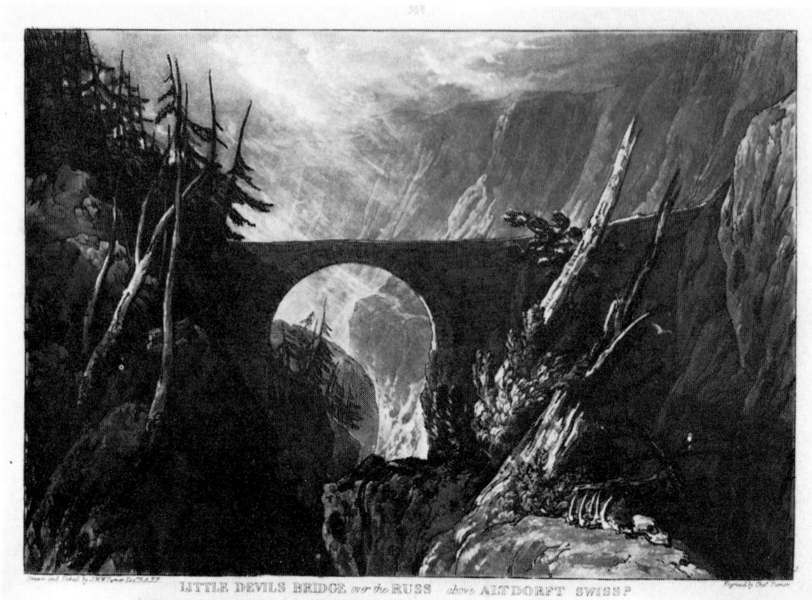

Plate 19 (MS) *Little Devils Bridge over the Russ above Altdorft Swiss*[d]

were there to illustrate Akenside's *Hymn to the Naiads.* The lightest naiad is placed so as to stress a Golden Section* – here much more firmly stated than in the watercolour.

Turner again uses strongly directional light in *Little Devils Bridge*, emphasising the tremendous sloping sides of the valley with parallel and opposing slashes of tree-trunks and shadows – massive forces to contain the beautifully thin arch carrying the roadway in as neat as possible an epigram of movement-across. And movement is implied in the whole treatment.

The Marine subject is based on the oil painting called 'The Leader Sea Piece' or, properly, *Guardship at the Great Nore, Sheerness*, now in the collection of Major General Goulburn.

As in many other sea pieces, Turner contrasts the lively speed of a small boat with the majestic immobility of a great ship at anchor. In the drawing and the etching these two vessels are the only ones, but in the final plate two more ships are added in a simple canon of the main theme. The lines of sun-rays and clouds repeat, on a different plane, the very sharp angle of the fore-and-aft-rigged boat.

*See Appendix

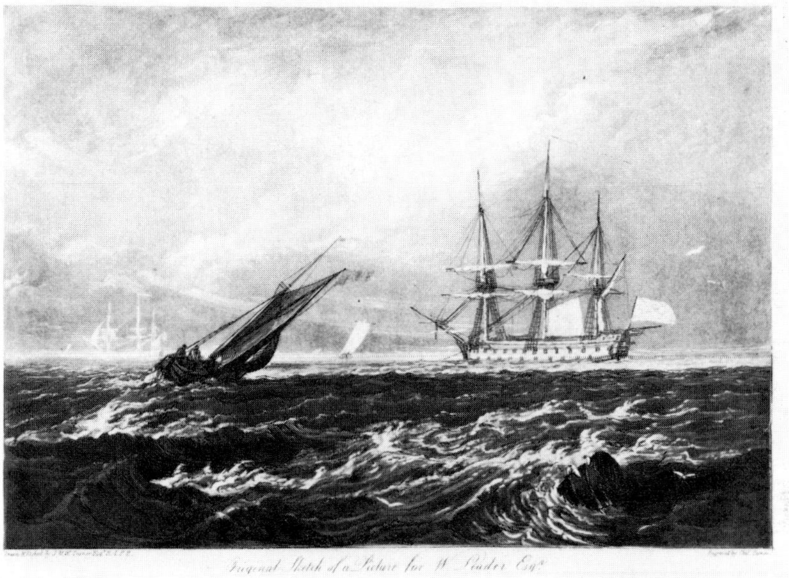

Plate 20 (M) 'The Leader Sea Piece'. 2nd published state
Below: 1st trial proof

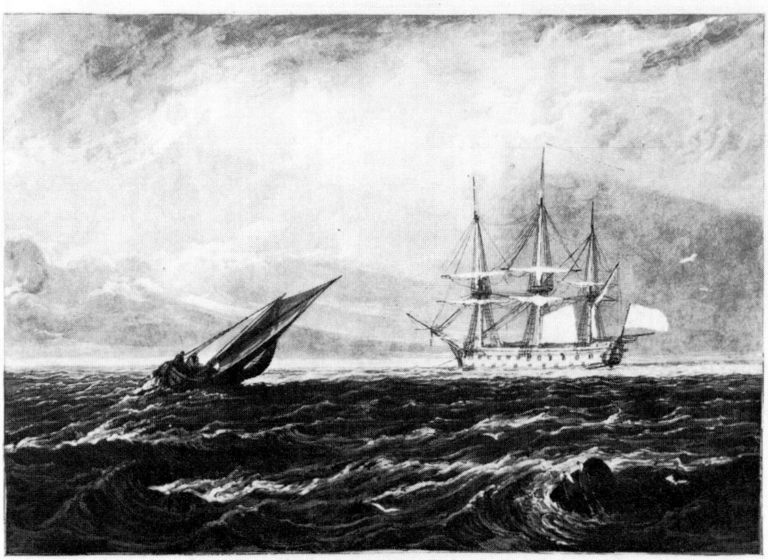

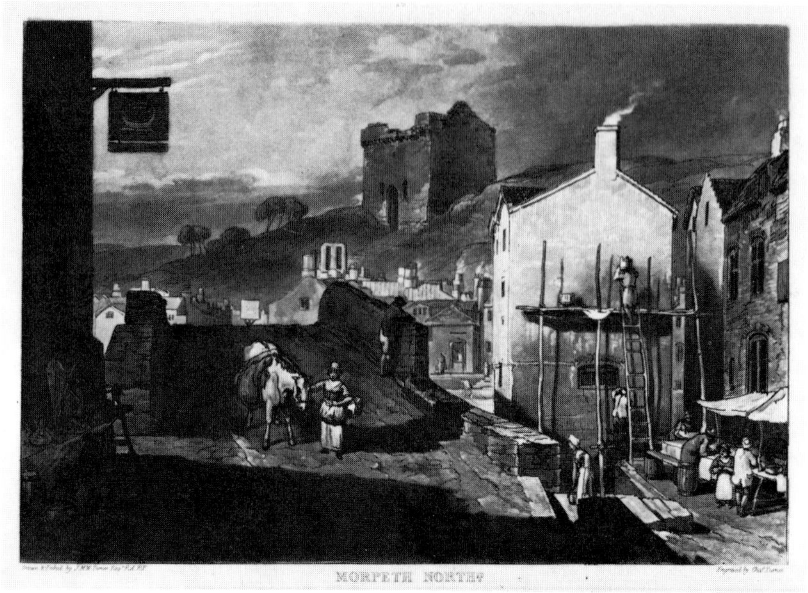

Plate 21 (A) *Morpeth North*[d]

Morpeth, on the face of it a somewhat boring piece of topography, is in fact an intriguing allegory of cyclic movement. On the bridge the woman and her pack-horse move towards us. To the right, we have *upward* movement (builders, smoke): in the background, movement *downward* (in the decay of the ruin) and *away* (the slope of the ground and the street disappearing beyond the bridge). The bridge brings us back to the start. The antique stall at the left (recycling?) and the little market on the right (distribution) form a similar triangle with the pack-horse (supply). At very nearly the centre of the picture area is the head of a motionless watcher who provides a pivot for the whole machine.

The large, early watercolour of *The Fall of the Clyde, Lanarkshire: Noon* is in the Walker Art Gallery, Liverpool, and a beautiful late oil painting, with all the elements of the composition transmuted and transposed, is across the Mersey at the Lady Lever Art Gallery, Port Sunlight.

PART 5 1 January 1811

Chiaroscuro

Disparity or contrast is the unifying theme of this set. The aimless behaviour and attitudes of the boys in *Juvenile Tricks* are set against the classical solemnity and beauty of the trees in the top half of the composition. The distant houses are also idealised. The picture as a whole is an essay in contrasts, light against dark and dark on light. Rawlinson says, severely: 'The comic element in the *Liber* could well be spared.' It is true that such genre pieces are not really Pastorals as Turner labels them: perhaps he was wrong to try to reach an unsophisticated audience. Sir David Wilkie, who became an RA in this year, was the popular, and very accomplished, master of genre, and Turner imitated him in several paintings of the early 1800s.

In *Coast of Yorkshire* the contrast is between the wild force of the sea and the static resistance of the rocks – further emphasised by the comparative peace of a pool protected by rocks in the foreground. By the actions of the figures a contrast is also made between danger and safety. In *Hind Head Hill* the portentously lit mound with its gibbet – this was a 'most villainous spot', according to Cobbett – contrasts with the cosily pastoral foreground. A wisp of rising smoke (as it happens, casually pointing a Golden Section) and a tiny moving coach, on the right, introduce small, 'real' movements into the total circulatory sweep of the composition.

The plate of *London from Greenwich* contrasts the Arcadian peace of the foreground with the distant fuss and commercialism of the city. The original picture (1809) was one of the first to be bought by Turner's lifelong friend and patron, Walter Fawkes, and it was a favourite subject with the painter. Studies of the deer are in a tiny sketchbook of 1808. * Contrast of light and shadow, as much as any linear perspective, is used to establish the relative distances very convincingly – even in the etching.

The remaining plate, the Elevated Pastoral 'Temple of Minerva Medica', employs antithesis in a more subdued way; and my theory becomes tenuous. The symbolism of the praying (oriental?) figure against the hollow, pagan temple beyond seems either obscure or trite, and the contrast of the fallen masonry and

*Wilkinson, 1974, p. 91.

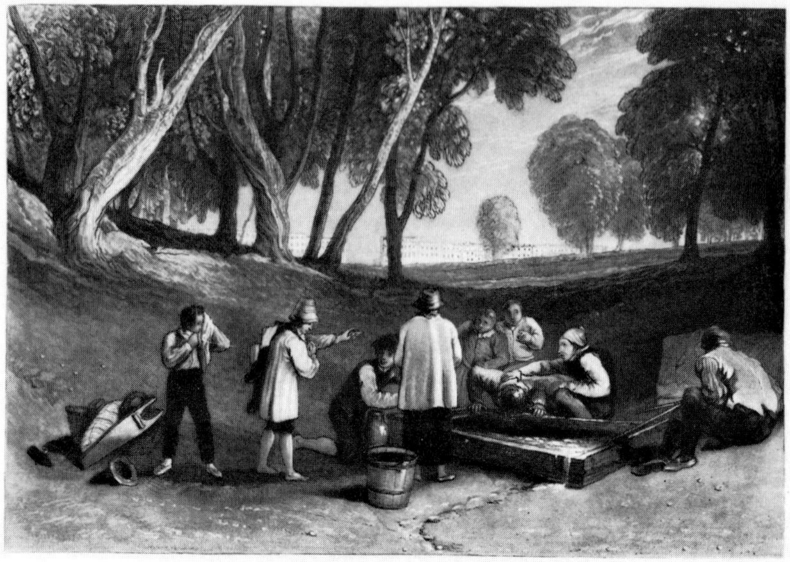

Plate 22 (P) *Juvenile Tricks*. A trial proof

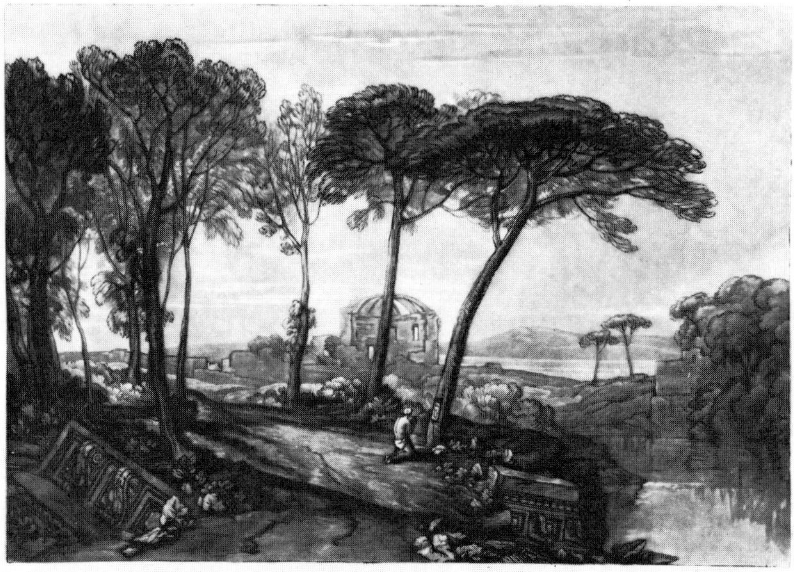

Plate 23 (EP) 'Temple of Minerva Medica', formerly known as 'Hindoo Worshipper'. A trial proof

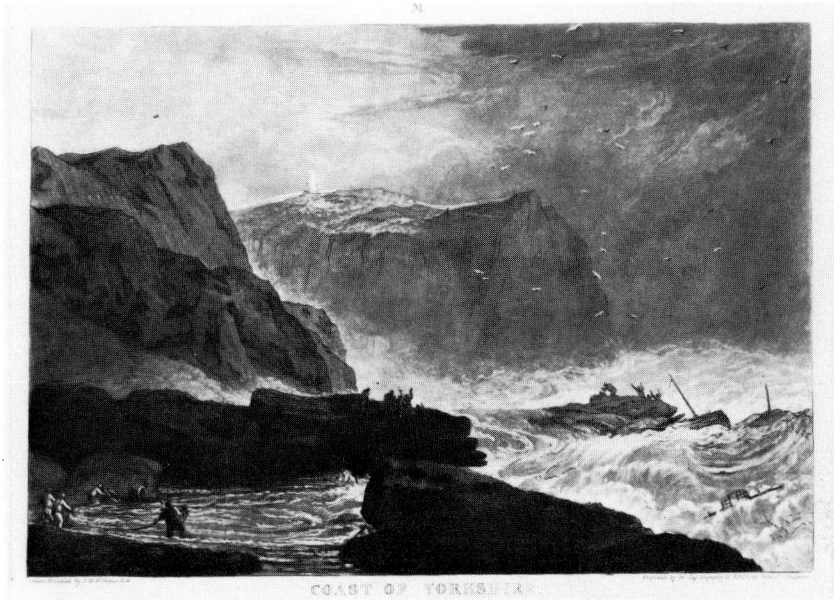

Plate 24(M) *Coast of Yorkshire, near Whitby*

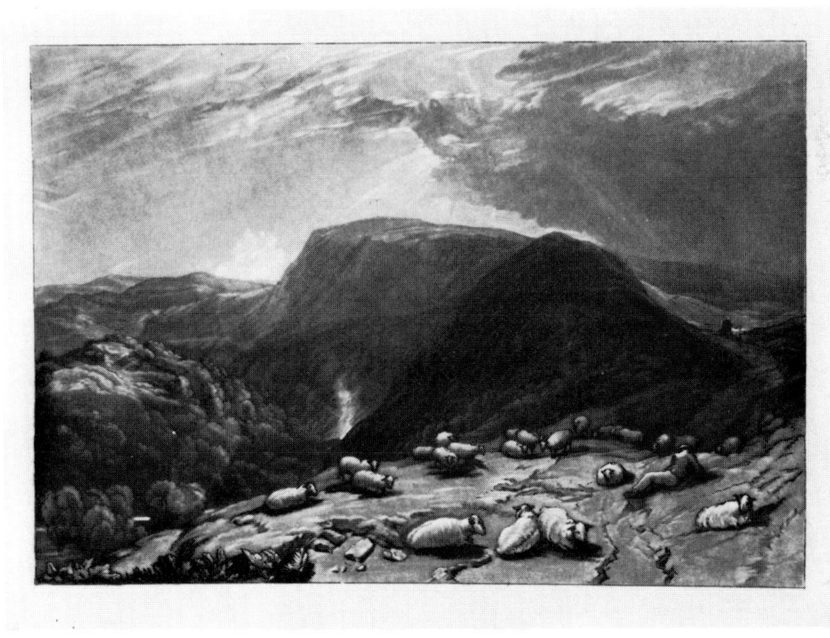

Plate 25 (M) *Hind Head Hill*, on the Portsmouth Road. A trial proof

the well-grown trees is too obvious to count. The picture is finely balanced if nothing else, and the contrast between dark foreground and light background might count in favour of the argument. Perhaps we should not expect Turner's leitmotiv to ring through each composition like a hammer-blow. He may have felt that the Elevated Pastoral was no place for extremes of contrast.

In the '*Liber* Notes 2' sketchbook, Turner listed the following subjects planned for Part 5:

Juvenile Tricks
EP *Chepstow*
Coast of Yorkshire
Hind Head
Spenser Fairy Queen

The last plate, published later in Part 7, is of unrelieved gloom, and would not have helped this 'contrasts' theme.

A

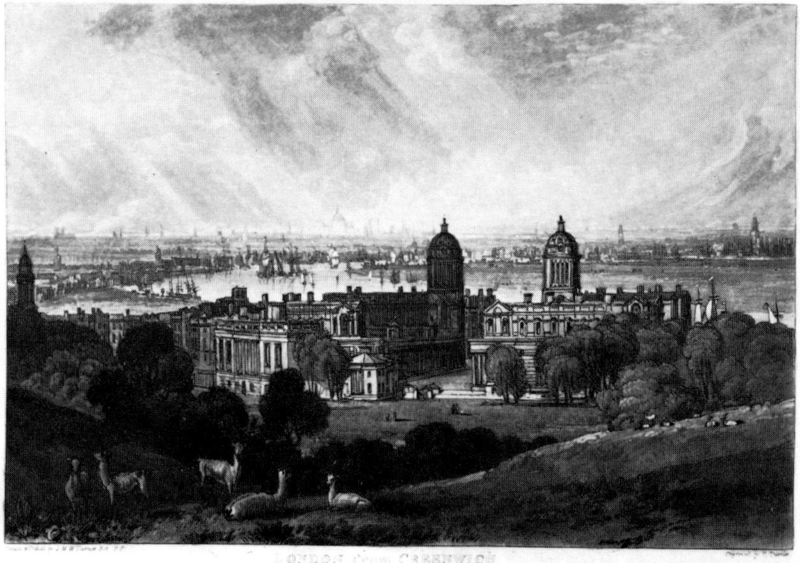

Plate 26 (A) *London from Greenwich*

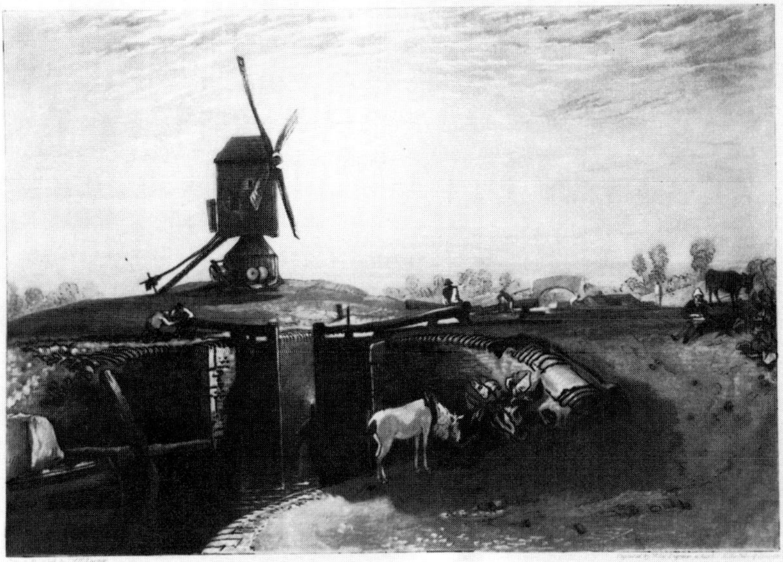

Plate 27 (P) 'Windmill and Lock'

PART **6** 1 January 1811

Angles and angling

Here Turner has put together five watery themes: two great rivers, one in its rapid stage, the other meandering; a canal; a mountain beck; and a shore scene. Water is thus the obvious unifying theme, but there is a less consistent theme of angular constructions, signalled in the first plate by the semaphore of the windmill (Plate 27). The heavy lock gates of this picture are repeated in the massive rudder of the boat under which the figures in *Marine Dabblers* play with their much smaller boats. The angles of the bridge at Lauffenbourgh are repeated all over the composition. A different mesh of angles encloses the fisherman in the glen in *Blair Athol*, even down to the criss-cross lines of his tartan costume. In Plate 28 the Wye approaches its junction with the Severn by means of a series of angular bends.

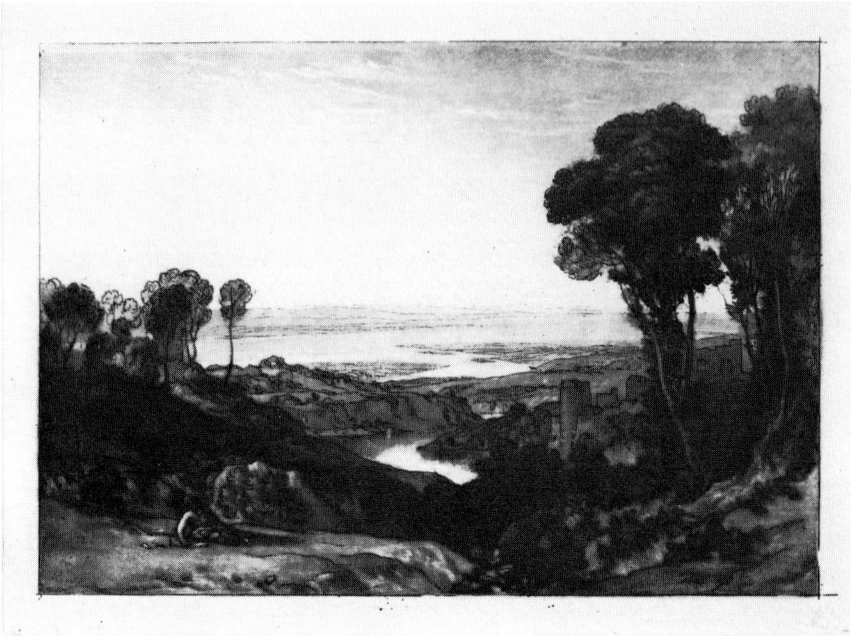

Plate 28 (EP) 'Junction of the Severn and the Wye'

The argument may be thought too slender. Only water is common to the five plates, and it makes for more difference than unity. Turner uses more forceful angles, more tellingly, elsewhere – in Part 4, for instance. In Part 6, however, the angles are used to build the compositions and are in each case essential components of the subject matter. They are cleverly deployed in axial, vertical, horizontal and cumulative dispositions. None of the designs relies on strong curves or vertical-horizontal grids. I feel that Turner is demonstrating that, while we now understand some of the basic elements of landscape (movement and contrast have been added to subject, pattern and geometry), we can still build our pictures from what we find in the scenes that confront us. We should not search for material to match some formula.

Something of this was in his mind when he painted the unprepossessing subjects of the 'Windmill and Lock' as a homage to Rembrandt, for it was the Dutchman's treatment of ordinary forms and objects that he most admired. He said, in the *Backgrounds* lecture previously quoted, that Rembrandt

> . . . threw a mysterious doubt over the meanest piece of common, nay, more, his forms, if they can be called so, are the most objectionable that could be

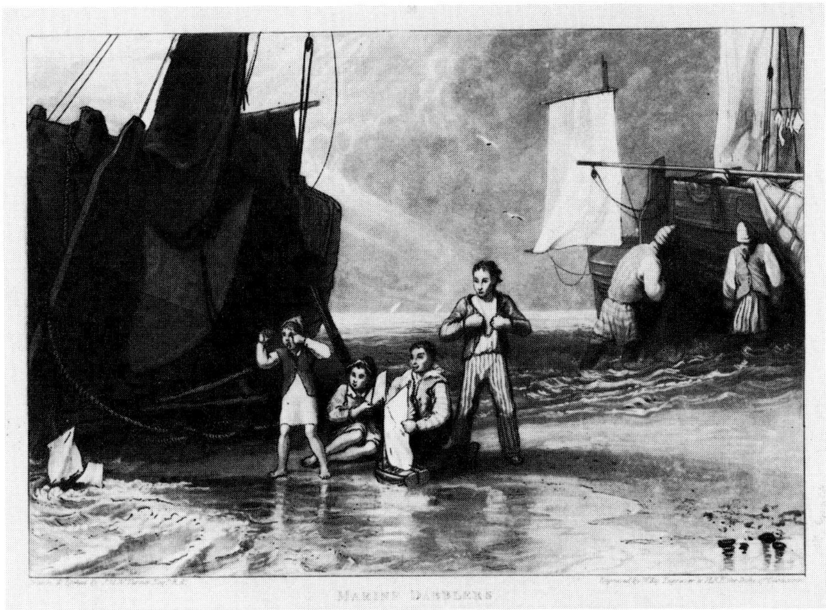

Plate 29 (M) *Marine Dabblers*

chosen . . . but over each he has thrown that veil of matchless colour, that lucid interval of Morning dawn and dewy light on which the Eye dwells so completely enthralled that it seeks not for its liberty.

But Turner does not succeed, in this plate. His lines are bitten too deep for any 'lucid interval' of light to be interposed. Said Ruskin: 'Turner has no joy of his mill. It shall be dark against the sky, yet proud, and on the hilltop; not ashamed of its labour, and brightened from beyond, the golden clouds stooping over it, and the calm summer sun, going down behind, far away, to his rest.' All of which, fanciful as it may be, makes the point. We may be somewhat relieved to find that a Golden Section passes between the lock gates, crossing another at the level of the canal bank, and elegantly supporting the whole arrangement of shallow, crossed angles. That must be why the 'Windmill and Lock' is so fascinating in spite of the crudity of the drawing – the 'objectionable forms'.

The oil painting entitled *Grand Junction Canal at Southall Mill* was exhibited in Turner's gallery in 1810 and is now in a private collection in England. The phrase, 'marine dabblers', turns up again in Turner's work, in a small autograph album which he used as a sketchbook in about 1830. He wrote the words under some miniature figures amongst some pages of not-too-serious seaside sketching. Clearly he had some fond memory, perhaps of his own childhood; and he still loved playing with boats.

Junction of the Severn and the Wye was sketched in watercolour in about 1798 (XXXVIII, p. 81) – see Wilkinson, *Turner's Early Sketchbooks*, 1972, where the 1801 pencil sketch of Blair Athol (LVI, 119a–120) is also reproduced. Turner used the composition again in a late oil painting now in the Louvre.

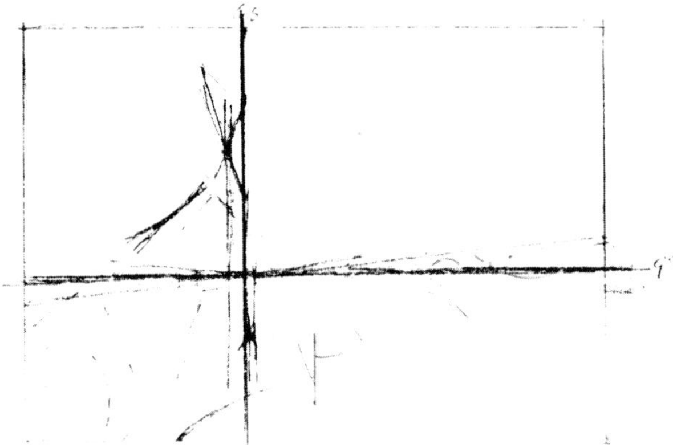

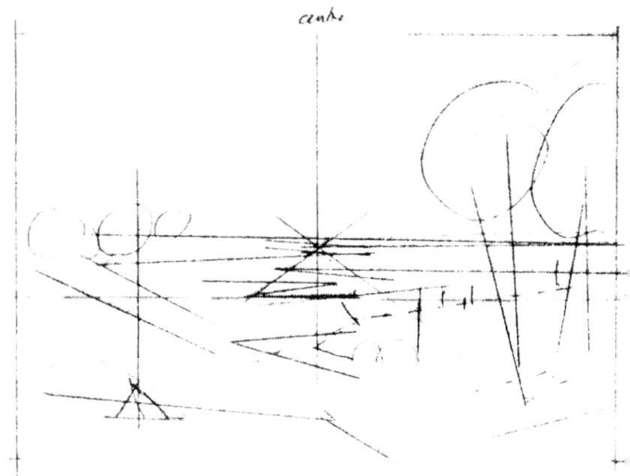

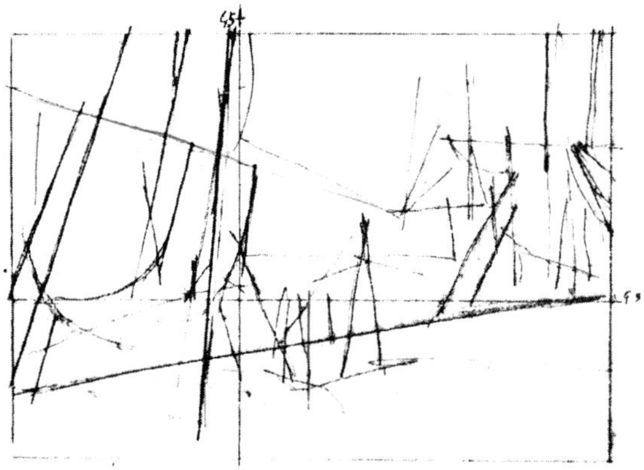

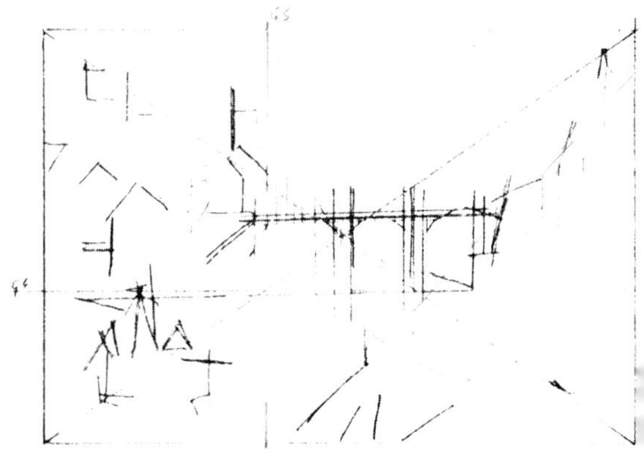

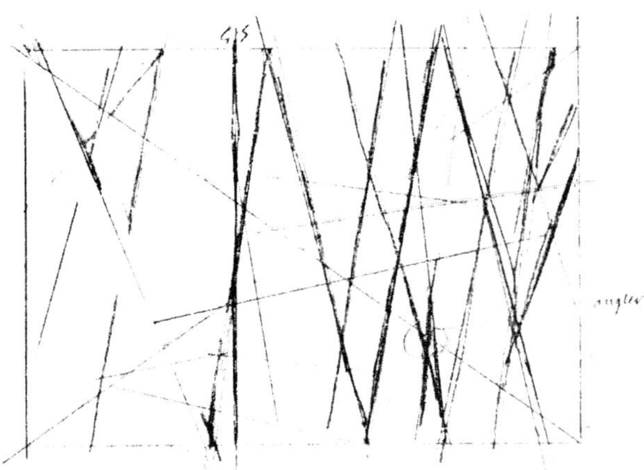

Some important constructional lines of the plates in Part 6

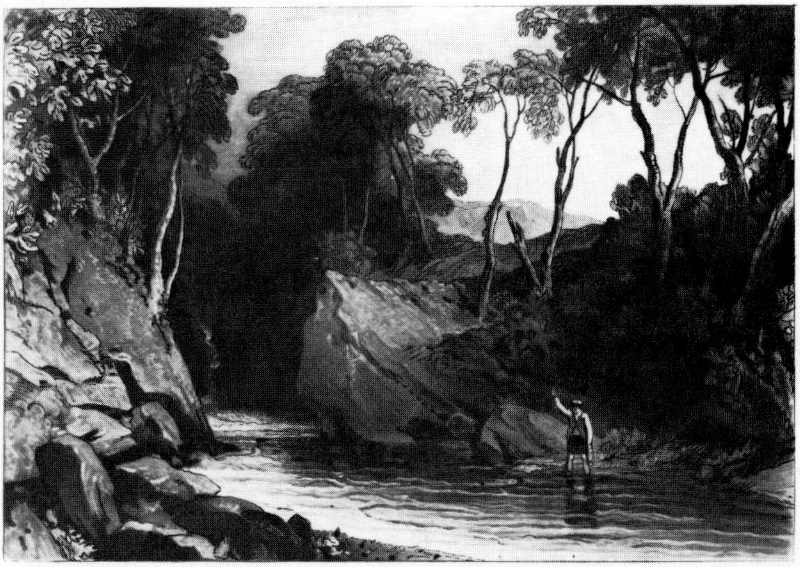

Plate 30 (M) *Near Blair Athol, Scotland.* 2nd trial proof

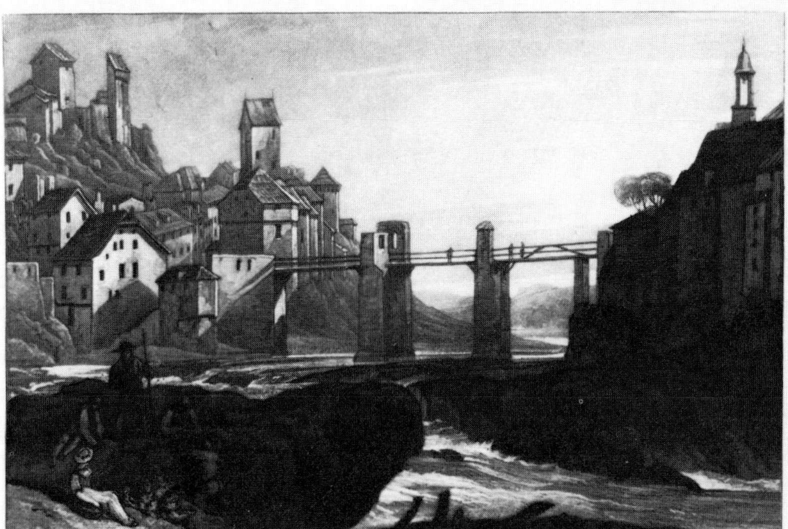

Plate 31 (A) *Lauffenbourgh on the Rhine.* 2nd trial proof

PART 7 1 June 1811

Fallacies of Hope

Jack Lindsay, in his *Critical Biography* of Turner, points to the great early 'vortex' picture, *Snowstorm, Hannibal crossing the Alps*, as the artistic resolution of an emotional and intellectual crisis. Lindsay traces, through a series of verses which Turner wrote in his sketchbooks, between 1808 and 1811, a 'sense of despair and disillusion that threatened to drag him down'. *Hannibal* was the first painting to which he attached a quotation from his mysterious epic poem, *The Fallacies of Hope*. This poem was never revealed as a whole, if indeed it was ever completed, but Turner continued to quote from it for verses for his pictures until 1850. It was fashionable in Turner's time to put 'explanatory' poetry in the Academy catalogues – a critic complained that they looked like anthologies. Even so, the generally morbid tone of Turner's quotations, and the idea that most of his important pictures were illustrations to a single, as yet fragmentary, but grand poem, is typical of him. Most of all, perhaps, the title itself is very revealing of this thematic drive, as Ruskin understood it (see the quotation on pages 42–3).

Something happened around 1811 which disturbed the course of his life – something that turned him away from the serene oil sketches and richly patterned watercolours on his home stretches of the Thames. It was something that sent him off on his travels in the summer, picking up the habit he had lost for eight years: something that deepened his dependence on his friend Walter Fawkes, of Farnley in Yorkshire.

Turner was building a villa in Twickenham, but he gave up his Hammersmith house before it was ready. In 1811–12 we find his address in the Academy catalogue as Sion Ferry House, Isleworth. From a sketchbook (XC) now redated to the early years of the decade, it appears that he had occupied Sion Ferry House for some years, probably using it as a studio while he lived at Hammersmith. Lindsay, in his *Sunset Ship*, writes: 'We search in vain among his public activities of 1811–12 for any clue' – to what did happen. But it seems natural to look to his private affairs for the explanation of a personal crisis. In February 1809 the diarist Farington noted that Turner's friend Callcott had told him that 'A Mrs Danby, widow of a musician, now lives with him. She has some children.' Two of the children were Turner's own. Eveline would have been at least nine years old and Georgianna a couple of years younger. That is all we ever hear of Sarah Danby, until 1820 when Turner mentions her in a will. The Reverend Trimmer, who became a friend of Turner's in about 1811 and subsequently gave us, indirectly, a good deal of information about his life in Twickenham, never mentioned her. If he had done, the biographer Thornbury, to whom he gave his reminiscences, would certainly not have ignored it.

The *Hannibal* picture, which was perhaps only an allegory of Napoleon's fall from heroism, and not a personal testament, was painted in the winter of 1811–12. In the summer of 1811 Turner had wandered on the Devon and Cornwall coasts collecting material for a book of line engravings to be published by W. B. Cooke, and composing verses (which the publisher didn't want). In the spring he had nine works in the Academy Exhibition, including an unusually wide selection of watercolours, among them *Chryses*, with a quotation from Pope's version of the *Iliad*:

> Disconsolate, not daring to complain,
> Silent he wander'd by the sounding main

In the plates of Part 7 of *Liber Studiorum*, which he was working on at this time, he concentrates, not on the construction of landscape compositions, but on their poetic content. His themes are close to the sentiment contained in the phrase, 'the fallacy of hope'.

The first and last plates are linked by the odd motif of a riven tree. Hope is the somewhat playful theme of *Young Anglers*, the subjects of which Turner, the enthusiastic fisherman, had seen near the Jew's Harp tavern in Marylebone Fields, not far from his house. The attitude of the knight, in *From Spenser's Fairy Queen*, is that of absolute defeat, as he crouches by the Cave of Despayre.*

In the beautiful design for *St Catherine's Hill* the strongly marked shadows and the plodding beasts and men form a frame for the light and sophisticated architecture, now ruined, of former hope and faith.

The martello towers on the south coast are monuments to the aspirations of Napoleon; in 1811, his hopes of adding Britain to his Empire were as empty as the bones of the rotting hulk which litters the foreground of Turner's engraving.

*The plate is not a literal illustration of any particular verses from *The Faerie Queene*, but this seems to be the incident which inspired the design. A late, unfinished painting, identified by John Gage as 'Cave of Despair' (Tate Gallery, no. 5522) bears no resemblance to the *Liber* subject.

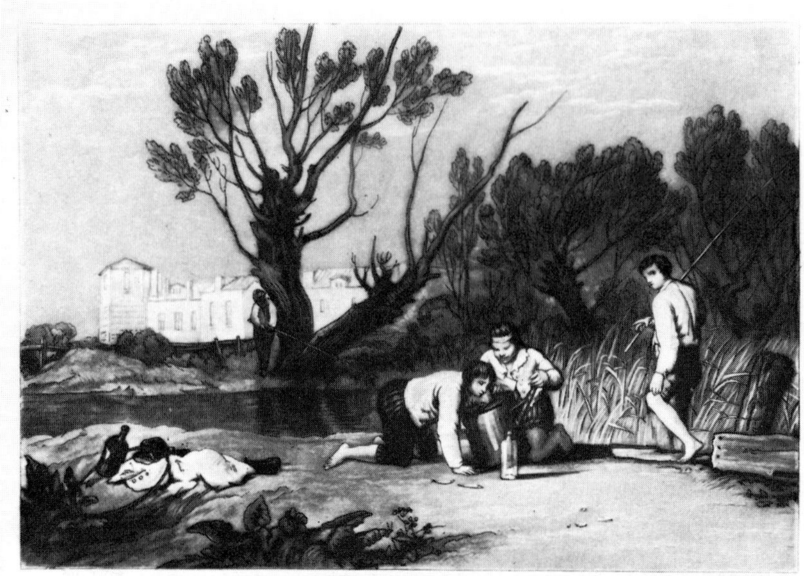

Plate 32 (P) *Young Anglers*

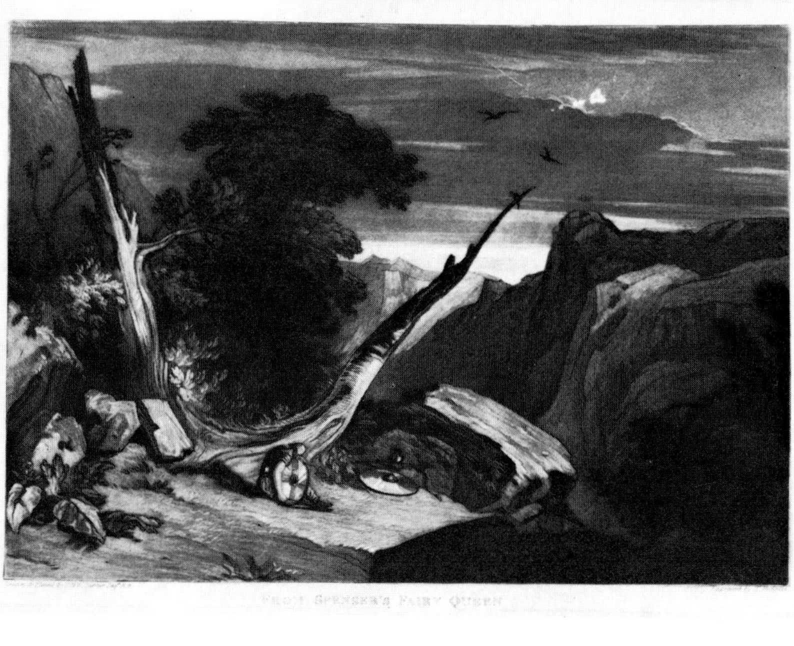

Plate 36 (H) *From Spenser's Fairy Queen*

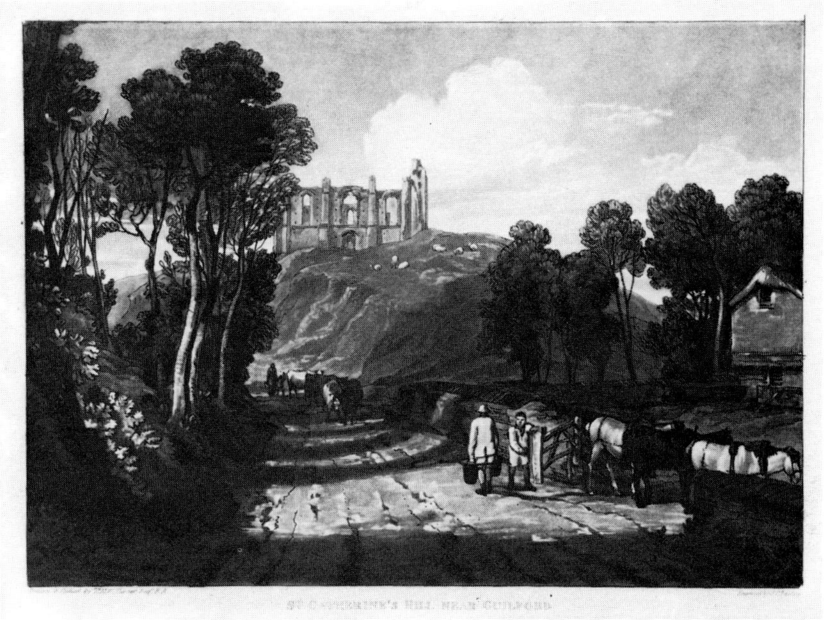

Plate 33 (EP) *St Catherine's Hill near Guildford*

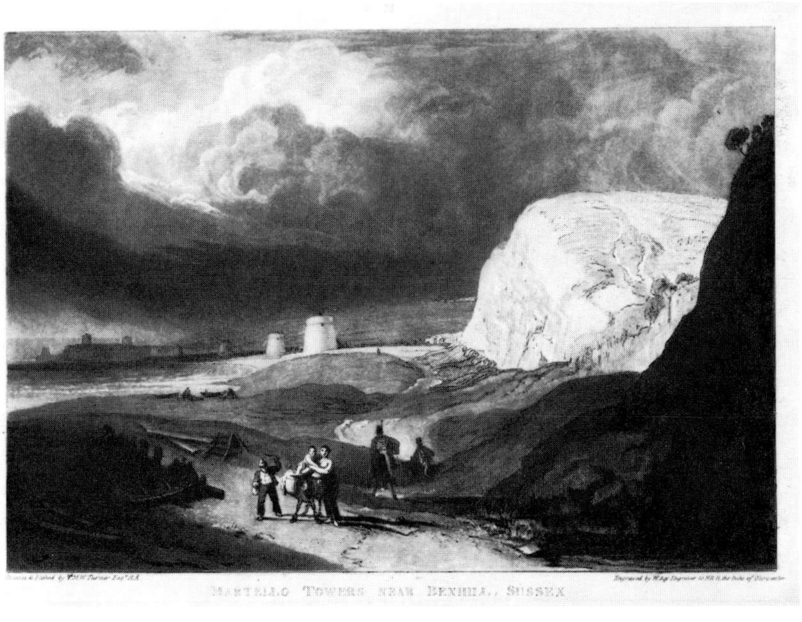

Plate 34 (M) *Martello Towers near Bexhill, Sussex*

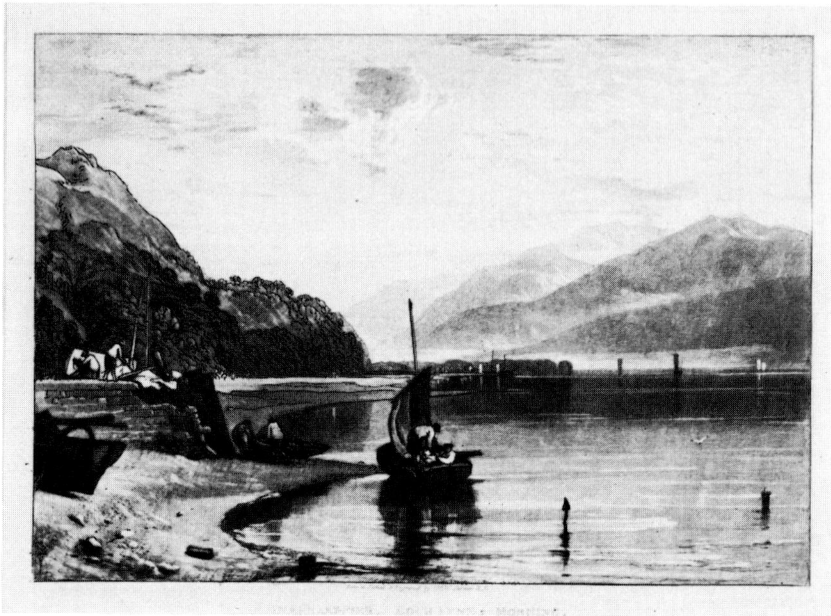

Plate 35 (M) *Inverary Pier, Loch Fyne, Morning*

The flickering light and shade, the dangerous-looking sky and, in case we missed the point, the off-duty soldiers, all speak of distant war.

Inverary Pier, Loch Fyne, Morning seems pervaded with melancholy, but the place has no associations, that I can find, with 'hope proved false'. Turner had explored Loch Fyne in 1801 as part of a rapid tour of the southern Highlands, and had done a watercolour of this subject. He did not penetrate far enough into the Highlands to find associations with the Young Pretender's hopeful and less hopeful travels, and I do not know whether at this time he had read Scott (whose *Minstrelsy* volumes were in print as well as his first three novels). Since he usually read up his backgrounds – he did in Wales, anyway, for his Caernarvon and Dolbadarn pictures of about 1800 – he may have known the story of the Appin murder, made famous later by R. L. Stevenson in *Kidnapped* and *Catriona*. At Inverary James Stewart of The Glen was condemned to death for the murder of Colin Campbell, 'The Red Fox'. Stewart was innocent but the members of the jury were Campbells.

Perhaps Turner simply wished to include in this set a picture which was in itself poetic, because of its mood and subject and not by association or story. Or perhaps, in 1811, he remembered his own hopefulness in 1801, as he returned to his mistress, Sarah, in London, and became, the next year, the youngest RA.

Inverary Pier was engraved as well as etched by the master. There is no drawing extant, but there are two versions of the etching. Many proof stages have been identified, and some of the later proof impressions were issued to subscribers. There are six states of the published plate, the last two being considerably reworked. See Gage, 1969, Plates 12 and 13, for what he describes as an amazing transformation. For all details of states, papers, inscriptions, see Finberg, 1924. Inverary appears again in Part 13: Plate 65.

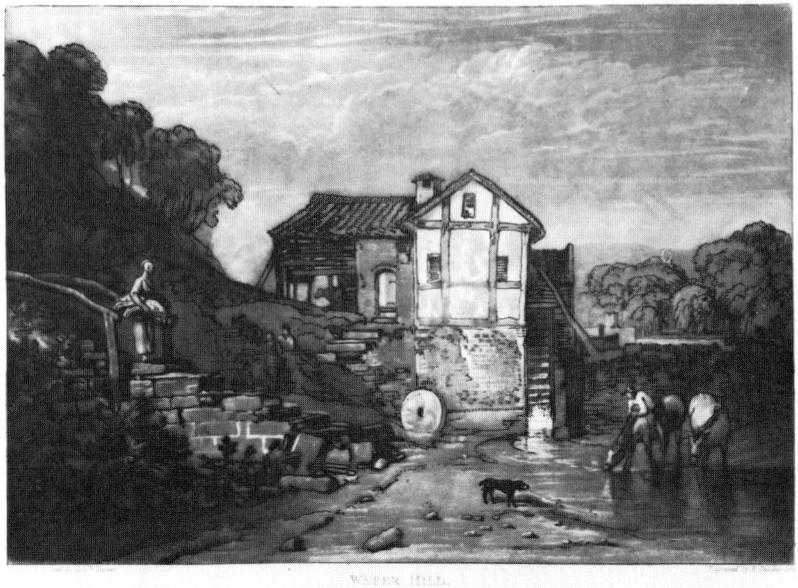

Plate 37 (P) *Water Mill.* 2nd state

PART **8** 14 February 1812

Steps in time and space

Each picture is a pattern of recession in space and sometimes a poem of recession in time.

The many parallel, stepped-back vertical planes of the decaying water-mill are set in a wooded valley which stretches back behind the mill. The stream flows forward to the picture plane.

The misty planes of the Elevated Pastoral 'Scene in the Campagna' and the placid sky recede in conventional, aerial perspective, aided by the strong, foreshortened rectangle of the tank in the foreground, thrown back by the dark trees and bank. The other dimension is temporal: Turner looks back to antiquity. His Roman scenery is, of course, second hand; he had yet to visit Rome.

In contrast, the perspective of 'Crypt of Kirkstall Abbey' is intimate. The drawing of the vaults is quite worthy of the Professor of Perspective. Ruskin

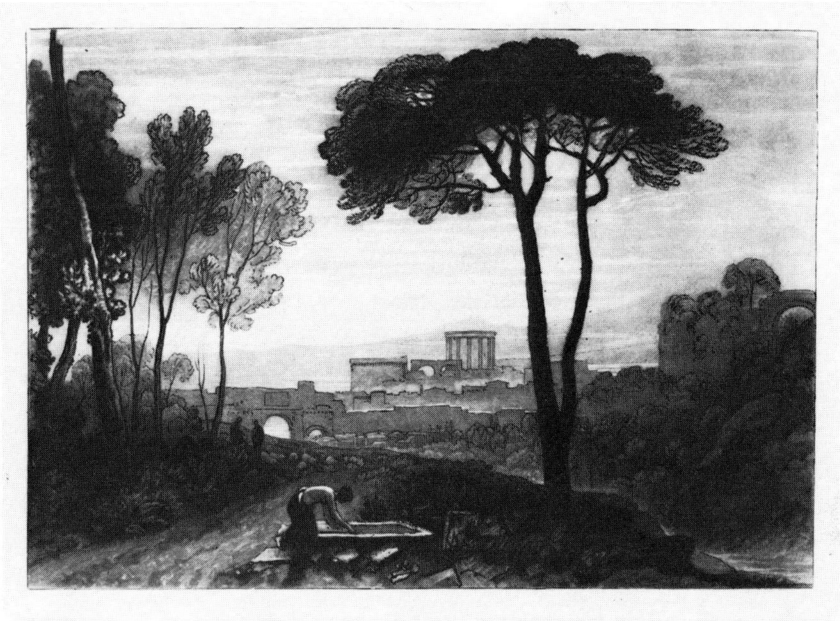

Plate 38 (EP) 'Scene in the Campagna', once called 'Hindoo Ablutions'. Turner called it 'Say's tall tree'. A trial proof

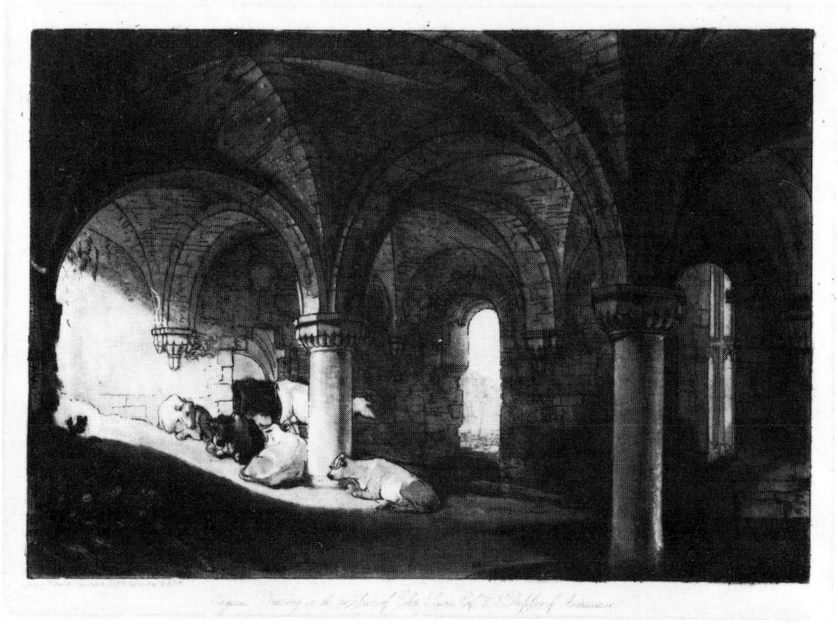

Plate 39 (A) 'Crypt of Kirkstall Abbey'

points to the moral, describing Turner's discovery on the Yorkshire moors, of 'Beauty and freedom and peace; and yet another teacher graver than these. Sound preaching at last here, in Kirkstall Crypt, concerning fate and life.'

Turner rightly included in this set one of his most original paintings, 'The Mildmay Sea Piece'. The painting itself is lost. Every detail of this composition, except perhaps the somewhat heavy group of objects in the left foreground, contributes to a dreamlike effect. The surface of the sea is used as an infinitely receding plane in the manner of the twentieth-century surrealists. The oddly converging lines of direction and the uneasy sense of scale depend, of course, on the subtle control of perspective.

The inviting perspective of a woodland path forms the setting for the Historical drama of *Procris and Cephalus*. There is a dual perspective in the story surrounding the two figures. Procris, who was spying on her lover from a thicket, is dead, her nearly blameless life behind her. Cephalus, through his own minor treachery the owner of arrows that cannot miss, has shot her by mistake, and faces the years of remorse ahead. It was the dawn goddess, Aurora, who was the rival of Procris; we may note the exact alignment of the fatal arrow with the direction of Aurora's early light through the distant trees on the right. Turner's perspectives are never earthbound.

Finberg (1924) identifies the water-mill as sketched between Hindhead and Guildford in the late autumn of 1807 when Turner was travelling from Portsmouth and recorded many scenes of rural life and labour. (See Ruskin's remarks in the quotation on pp. 42–3.) *Hedging and Ditching* (Plate 47) is another less than cheerful subject originating from this sketchbook (Turner Bequest C). Other sketchbooks of this period (XCVI and XCVII) contain rustic figures bending to their labours, and costume notes on the rural poor.

The mill has a superficial, perhaps accidental, resemblance to a view of Pembury Mill in two watercolours of 1795–6, in the Victoria & Albert and the British Museums respectively. The Pembury Mill, of Plate 12 in Part 3, by contrast, has a busy, thriving atmosphere with no hint of gloom or depression.

'Crypt of Kirkstall Abbey' is based on a watercolour as its caption explains, and the picture is still in Sir John Soane's Museum. Described as *Refectory of Kirkstall Abbey*, it was first exhibited in 1798. There are sketches of the crypt in the 'North of England' sketchbook (XXXIV). The plate was 'Drawn Etched & Engraved by I. M. W. Turner Esqr. R.A.P.P.' (Turner did not permit himself the use of the non-Latin J in the *Liber*).

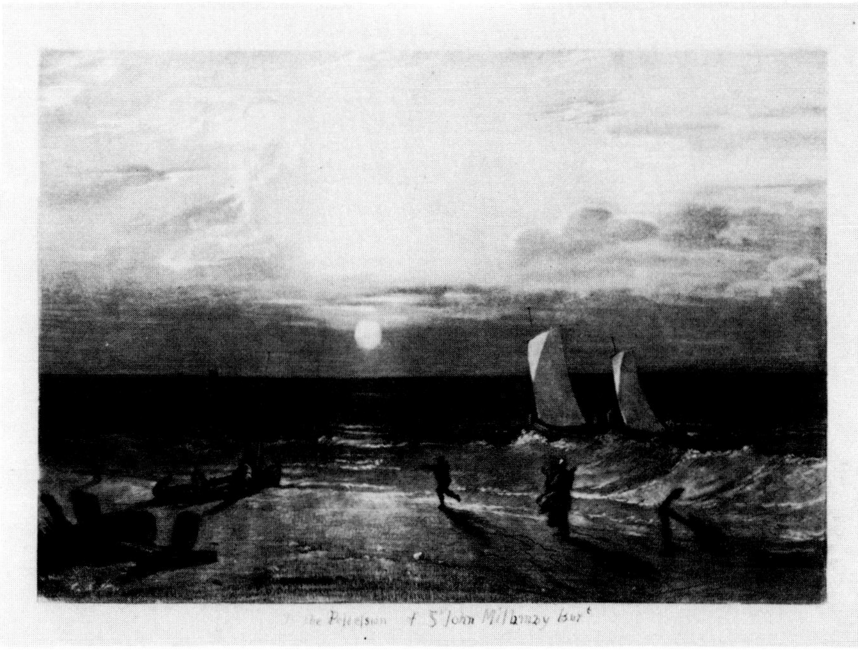

Plate 40 (M) 'The Mildmay Sea Piece'

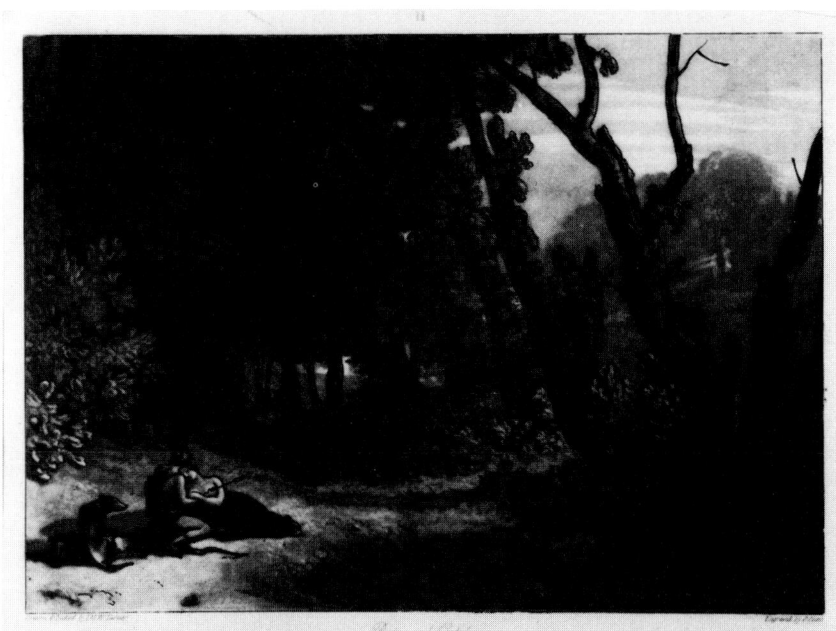

Plate 41 (H) *Procris and Cephalus*

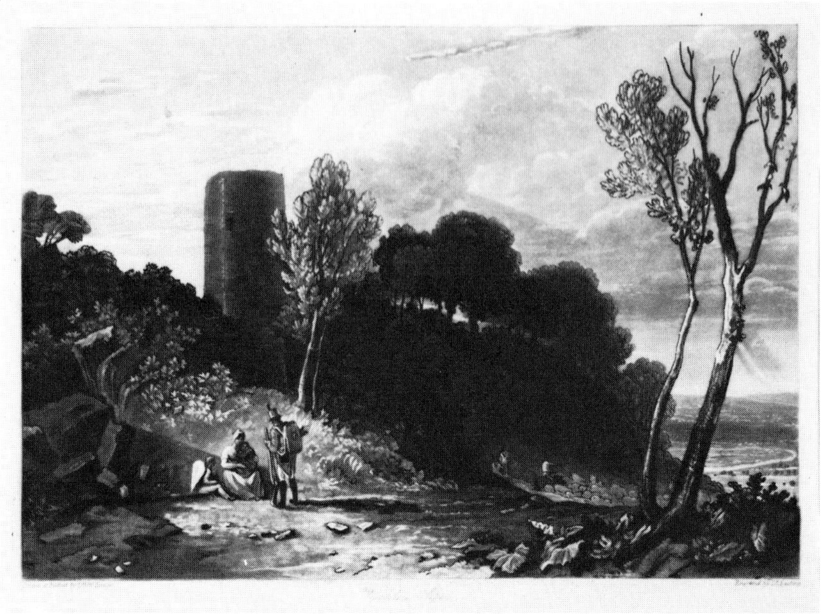

Plate 42 (P) *Winchelsea, Sussex*

PART **9** 23 April 1812

Action offstage

This set of examples demonstrates the usefulness of potential action, or movement beyond the picture frame. In the first two plates we have roads leading outwards. The soldier shown in *Winchelsea* tells his story, and the road turning in the distance – and the light – bring us back to the ruined watch-tower with its much older story.

A similar group of figures is in the foreground of the consciously archaic 'Bridge and Goats': a woman and child, with a man this time pointing histrionically. This was the aquatinted plate by F. C. Lewis originally intended for an earlier part – we may guess, for Part 1 (bridges). This is a classical composition and not to be disturbed by romantic speculations.

Calm, a most impressive plate which Turner himself took from soft-ground etching to aquatint and mezzotint through no less than fourteen different states, is an almost abstract evocation of potential movement. He achieves a Poussin-

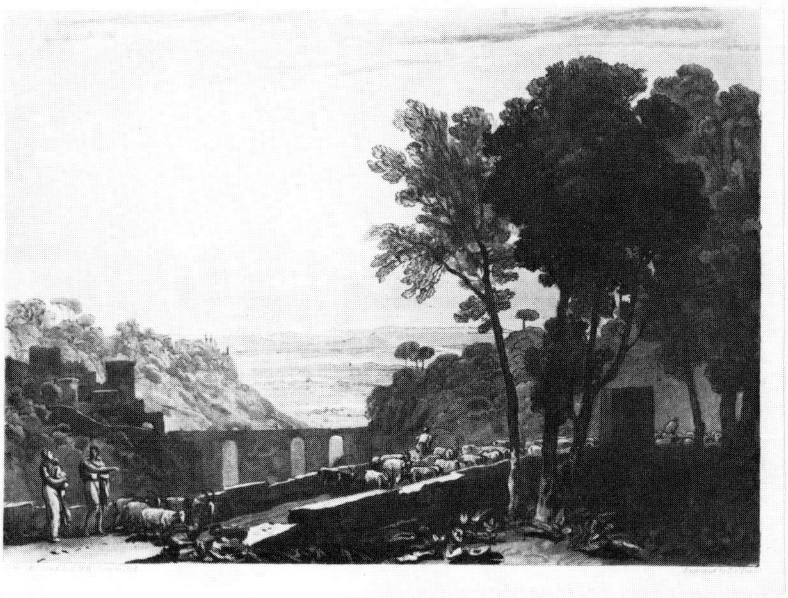

Plate 43 (EP) 'Bridge and Goats'

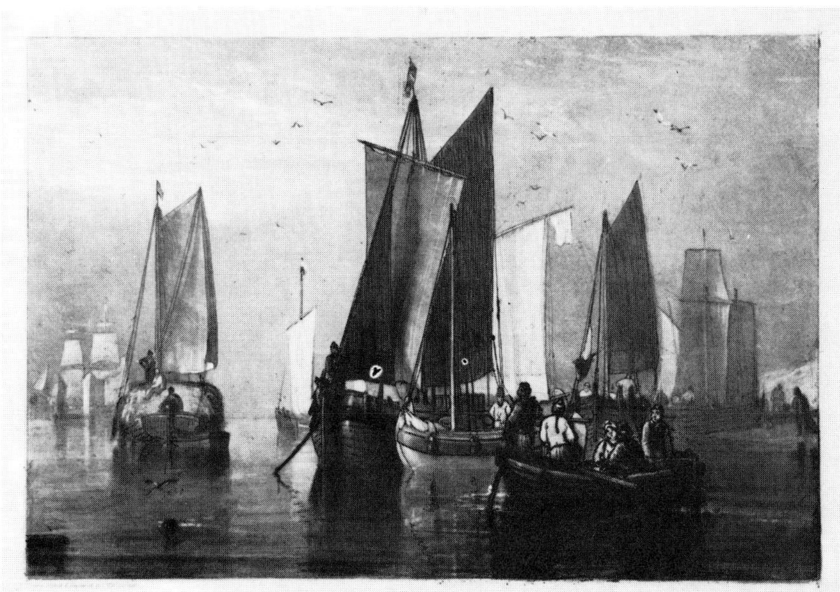

Plate 44 (M) *Calm*

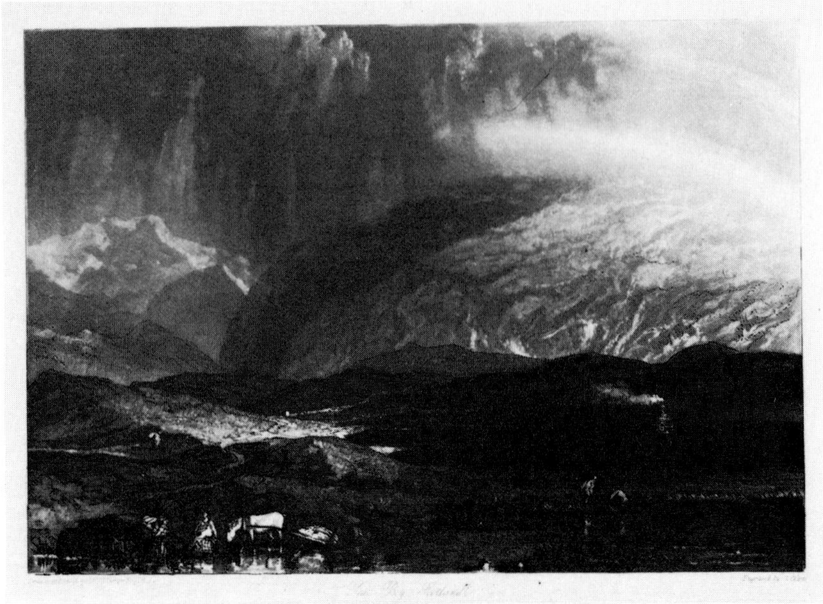

Plate 45 (M) *Peat Bog, Scotland*

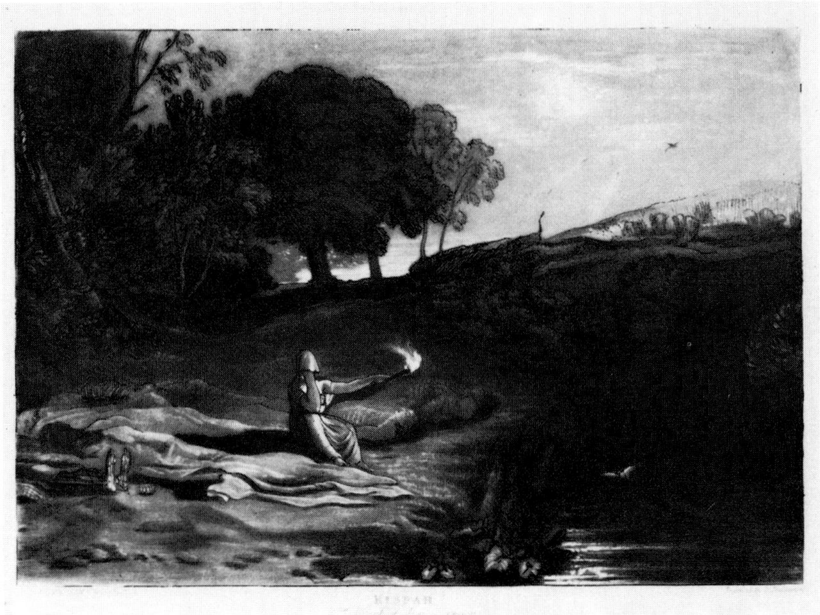

Plate 46 (H) *Rispah.* Opposite: The soft-ground etching for *Calm*

esque effect of motionless circulation. 'Calm' was the original title on the sketches for *Sun Rising through Vapour*. The *Liber* plate can be seen as a continuation of the theme finally worked out in *Dort*, 1818.

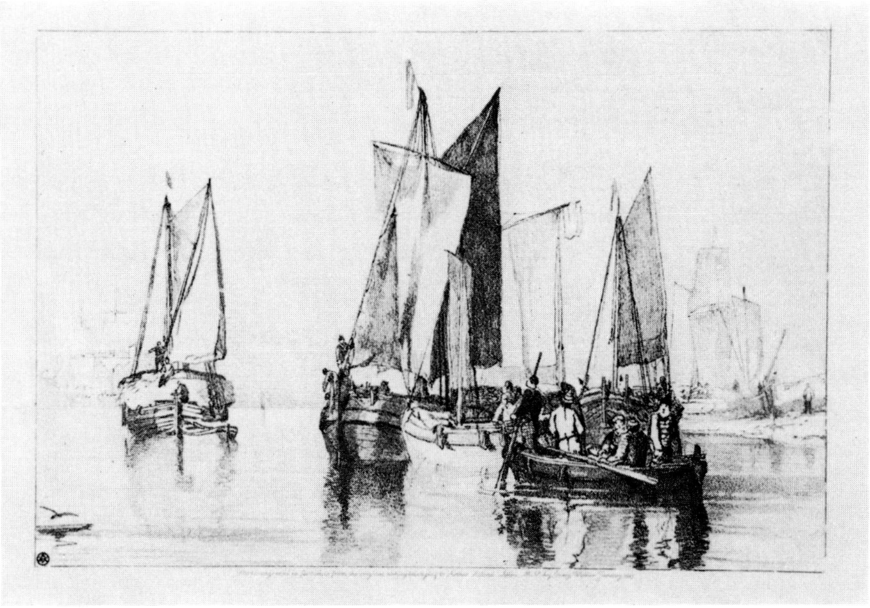

Peat Bog, Scotland is one of the finest of the published plates. It is a picture, not just of a storm in the mountains, but of the *movement* of a storm across a mountain valley. Turner uses many lines of force extending out of the picture, downwards and upwards as well as across, and uses them with the greatest mastery. The plate is entirely relevant to the theme of this group, but it is more: a great picture.

In *Rispah* little attempt is made to support the 'action' by formal or symbolic means. The woman's dreadful vigil by the corpses of her sons, while the crops ripen to harvest, is apparently sufficiently well known.* Turner, true to the Renaissance tradition, does not even attempt a biblical landscape, and contents himself with a mere glimpse of a cornfield. The torch held by Rispah is for warding off the beasts of the field, and the small gleaming object on the ground is the crown of the House of Saul.

An oil painting exhibited in 1808, *A subject taken from the Runic superstitions – unfinished*, which is obviously of the same subject, is more fantastic. The *Encyclopaedia Biblica* tells us that the story of Rispah may be unhistorical: 'Winckler suspects mythological affinities.'

*The caption to the plate gives the reference: Samuel ii, 21.

PART **10** 23 May 1812

The land

Problems of scale appear to be Turner's main interest in this part.

Hedging and Ditching is like a photograph that hasn't quite succeeded. The scene was in fact sketched from life during the journey back from Portsmouth in October 1807, when Turner made many sketches, notable for their spirit of realism, of workers in the countryside. He had discovered the melancholy of rural England, peopled as it then was by labourers kept just above starvation level by the Speenhamland system of family allowances. Several other *Liber* plates originated from the sketchbooks of autumn 1807, including *Water Mill* (Plate 37) and *St Catherine's Hill* (Plate 33). The figures in this plate are certainly not mere staffage; and they are as large in the landscape as they could be without taking it over and converting it into genre. The sheep are unfortunately out of scale with the people. The woman is poised, lumpishly, on a Golden Section, but appears to have no other function.

Turning to *River Wye*, we experience a sudden jolt of scale. The angle of view is the same, but everything in the picture is smaller. Again there is the difficulty with the comparative sizes of beasts and men – even allowing for the largeness of the cows bred at that time (for their ability to survive on muddy commons).

In *Chain of Alps*, closely based on a sketch of 1802 (LXXV, p. 26), the scale is immense, but is managed skilfully by conventional drawing methods. The next plate, *Mer de Glace*, is also Swiss and mountainous. Here there are no human figures in the foreground and little use can be made, either, of aerial perspective. Turner relies on line, alone almost, in attempting to build up the idea of colossal size. The bird in the left foreground was added only in the final proof to disguise a deeply etched mark, and does little or nothing to establish a point of reference. The resemblance to the Swiss drawings of Francis Towne may not be entirely accidental, for Towne held an exhibition in London in 1805.

The final plate of this part, *Rivaux Abbey*, employs a human figure – by a normal-sized doorway – to establish the scale of the whole. Even so, the recession to the parallel arcaded wall is not emphatic, and Turner seems more concerned with the harmony and modulation of the various arches than with the more mundane business of 'real' scale.

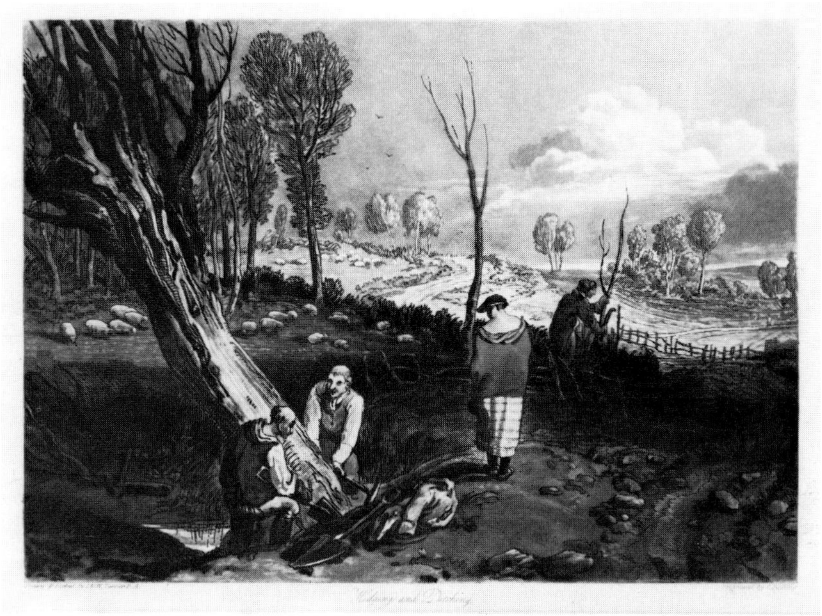

Plate 47 (P) *Hedging and Ditching*

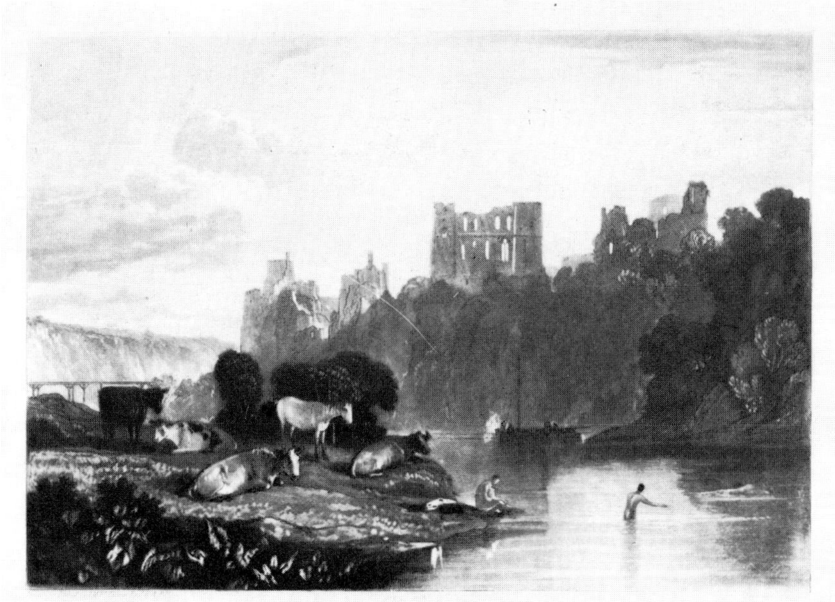

Plate 48 (EP) *River Wye*

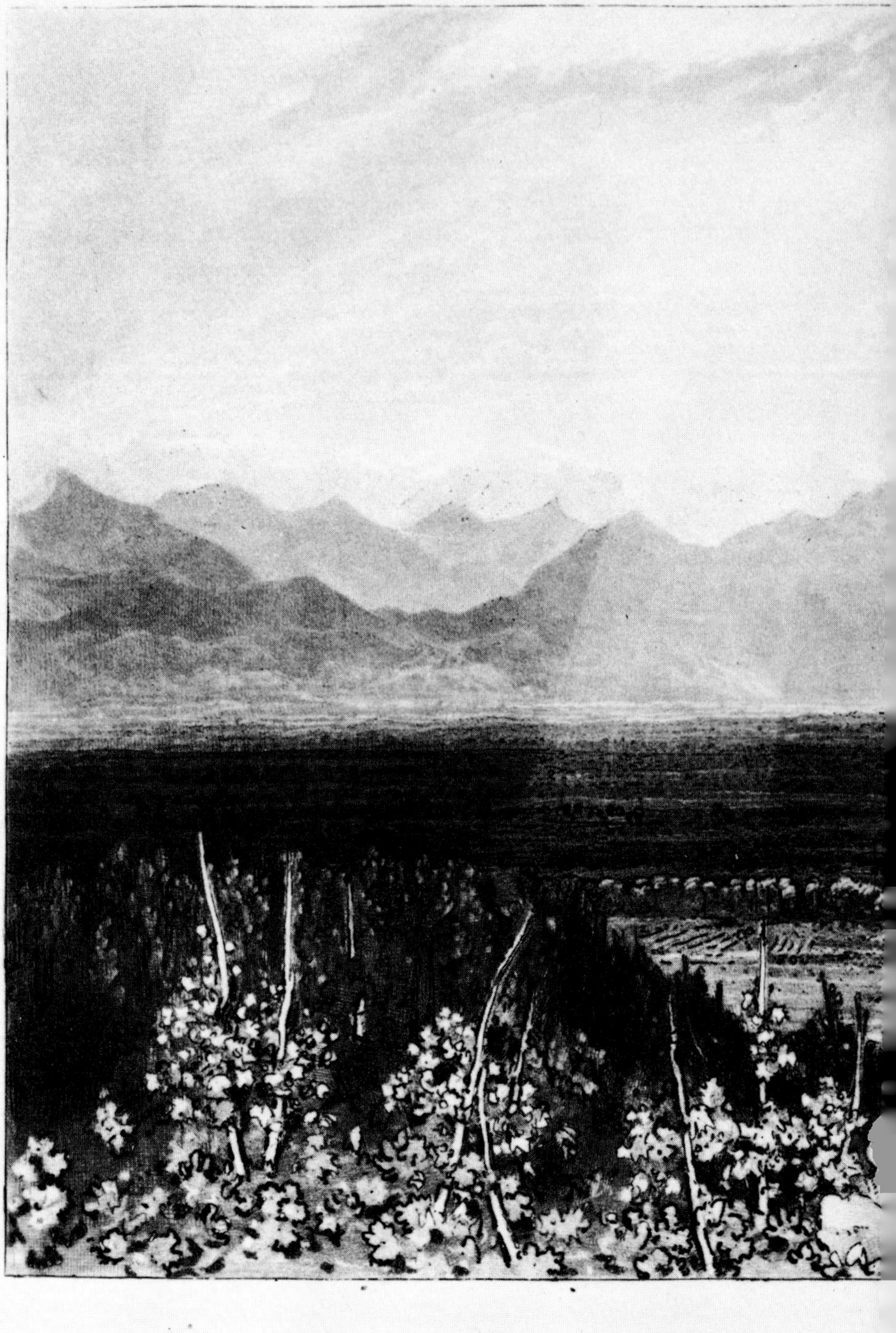

Plate 49 (M) *Chain of Alps from Grenoble to Chamberi*. A late trial proof. Actual size

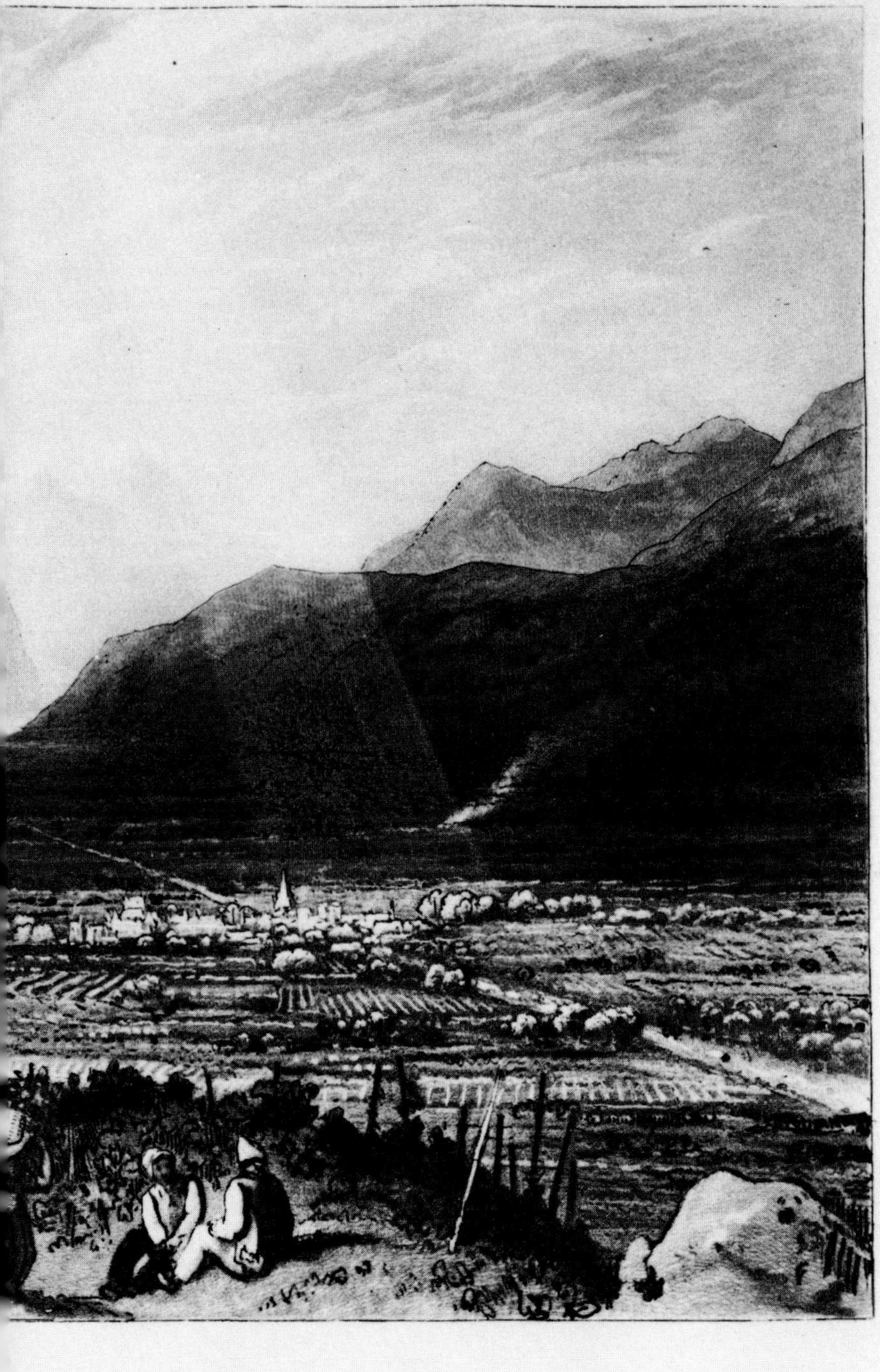

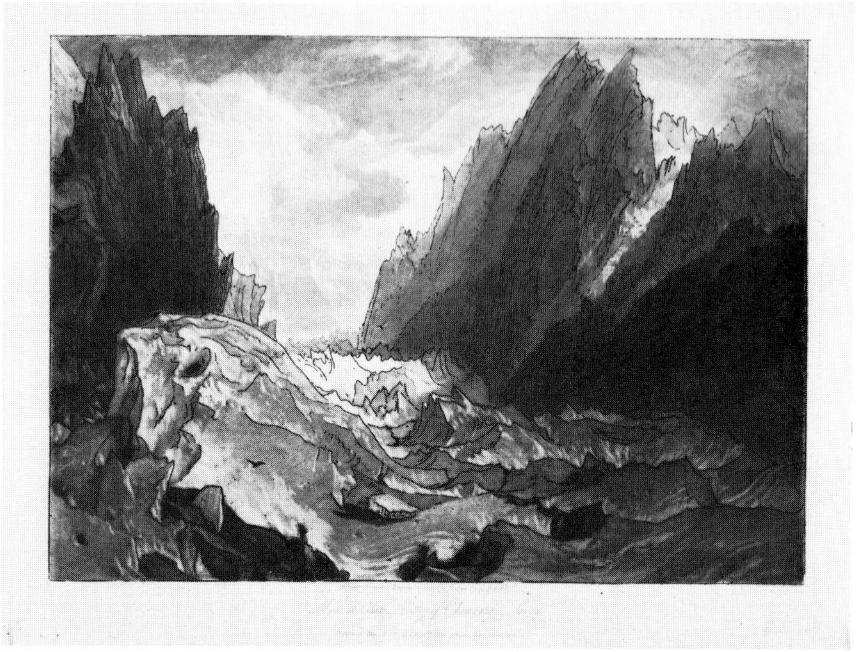

Plate 50 (M) *Mer de Glace – Valley of Chamonix – Savoy*

Apart from scale, Part 10 deals with the problem of what is now called 'land-use' – highly relevant to landscape art. The men in *Hedging and Ditching* are at work on the very process by which the commons and wilderness were converted to intensive livestock producton. The sheep now occupy what was once a very useful (to the commoner) bit of woodland – the source of wood for building and fuel, game, and the all-important 'mast' for fattening pigs. Turner shows us, beyond the dark foreground, a typical piece of common, half heath, half woodland, and unfenced.

In *River Wye* he illustrates the harmony and peace of the older system, symbolised by the feudal ruins. In *Chain of Alps* the peasantry work every foot of fertile soil, richly textured in the drawing, to the foothills of the Alps. A natural spotlight picks out the village as the centre of this highly productive area. In *Mer de Glace* there is no land-use at all, obviously.

Rievaulx was one of the richest of the Yorkshire Cistercian monasteries (Fountains was the largest, with up to 20,000 sheep on some of the earliest enclosed land in Britain). The picture symbolises the way in which previous ages have altered the landscape. Here the trees, which once, before the sheep, completely forested the moors, are creeping back into the ruined cloister.

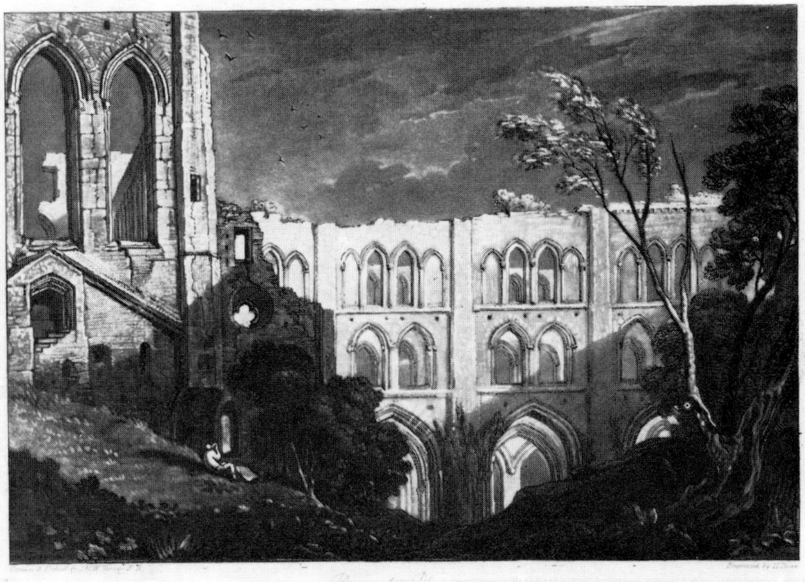

Plate 51 (A) *Rivaux Abbey, Yorkshire*. 4th state

Fifty plates of *Liber Studiorum* were now completed, constituting Volume One. Loyal subscribers were presented with the title page, illustrated on p. 43.

PART **II** 1 January 1816

The human environment

After a pause of nearly four years, Volume Two began with a continuation of the theme treated in the last part of Volume One: man in the landscape. It is not agriculture, but the fundamental situation of man which now concerns us – his opposition to, or harmony with, the forces of nature.

Solway Moss, or, as Rawlinson tells us, Lochar Moss on the Solway, was typical of many such morasses still all over Britain in the nineteenth century. In this plate the herdsman raises his arms, apparently to signal his victory in bringing the herd safely across, or perhaps as a warning to the traveller to stop. The danger and possible terror of the place is emphasised by one of Turner's tremendous skies, beautifully handled in the drawing and well translated by the engraver, Lupton, who became a fine interpreter of Turner's darker moods.

In 'Solitude' the human figure is, of course, at rest and at peace with the surroundings. A castle – again the feudal symbol – looms in a warm mist. The

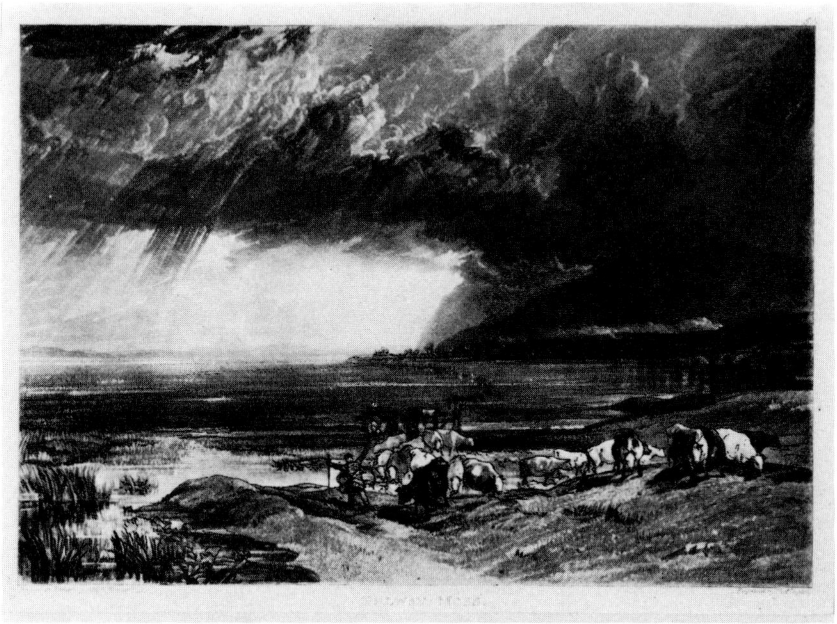

Plate 52 (P) *Solway Moss.* A finished proof

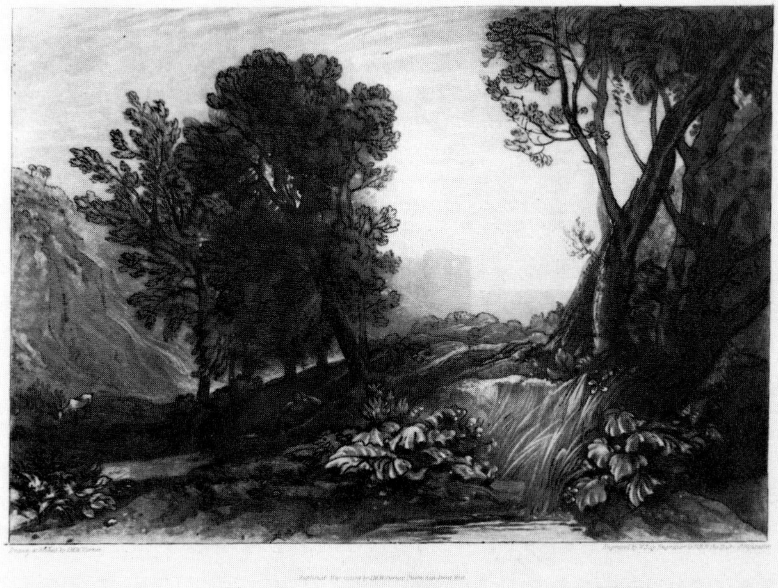

Plate 53 (EP) 'Solitude'

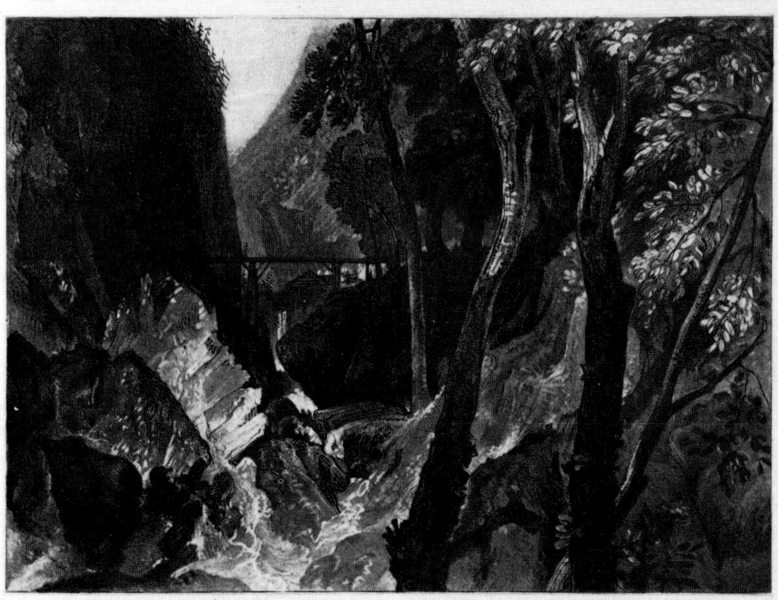

Plate 54 (M) *Mill near the Grand Chartreuse – Dauphiny*

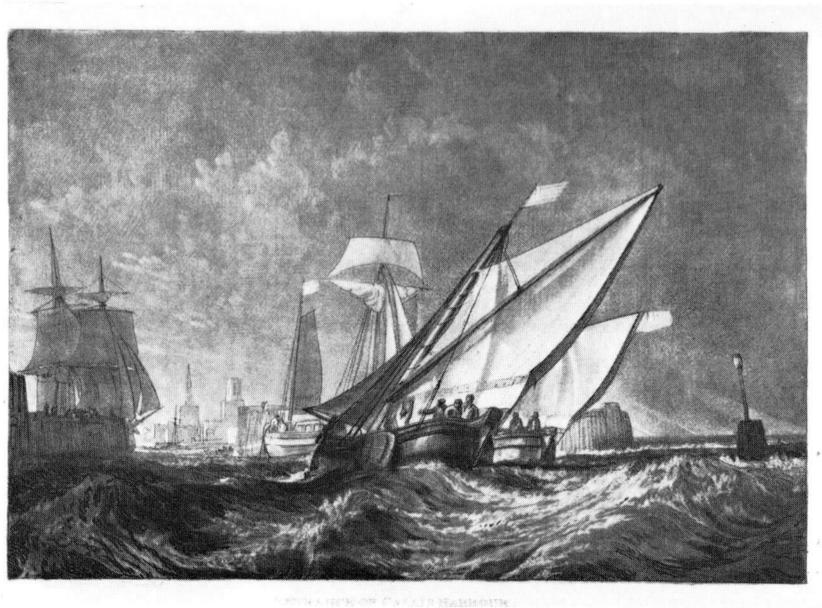

Plate 55 (M) *Entrance of Calais Harbour*

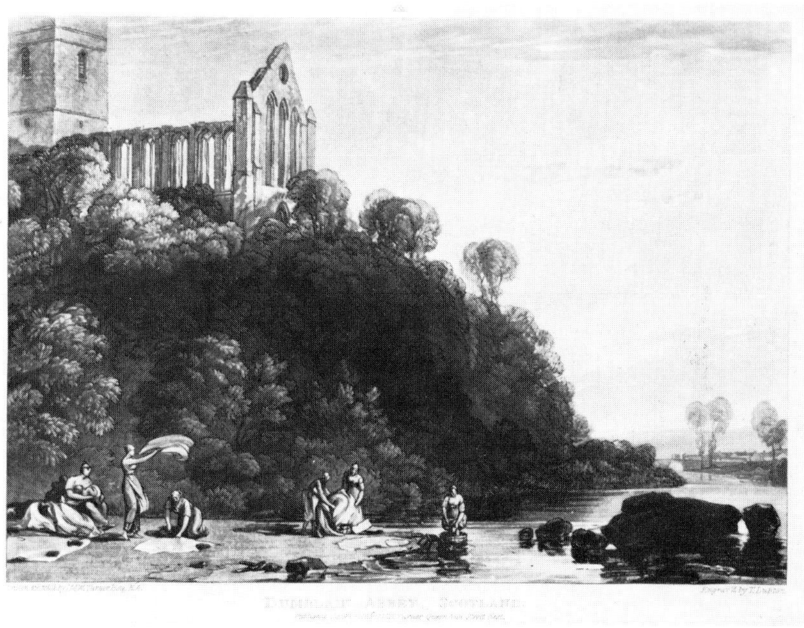

Plate 56 (A) *Dumblain Abbey, Scotland*

engraving, by William Say, is a little spoilt by a slimy passage in the foreground. The composition of this plate was revived in a much later, very atmospheric painting, 'Sunrise . . .' (Tate Gallery, no. 1985). *Mill near the Grand Chartreuse* stands for man's harnessing of a natural force – again very harmonious, and a fine drawing by any standard. In *Entrance of Calais Harbour* the contrast is made between the wild wind and sea, and the dignified serenity of the man-made harbour – significantly emphasised in the engraving as compared with the painting* which was the basis for the plate. In *Dumblain Abbey* the feature of the landscape, a cliff above the river, is crowned by a noble piece of medieval building. Finally, the women washing in the shallows stress the human element, at peace in quotidian toil.

In these landscapes Turner exploits diagonals in the composition – in the last two, very vigorously.

*In the Frick Collection, New York.

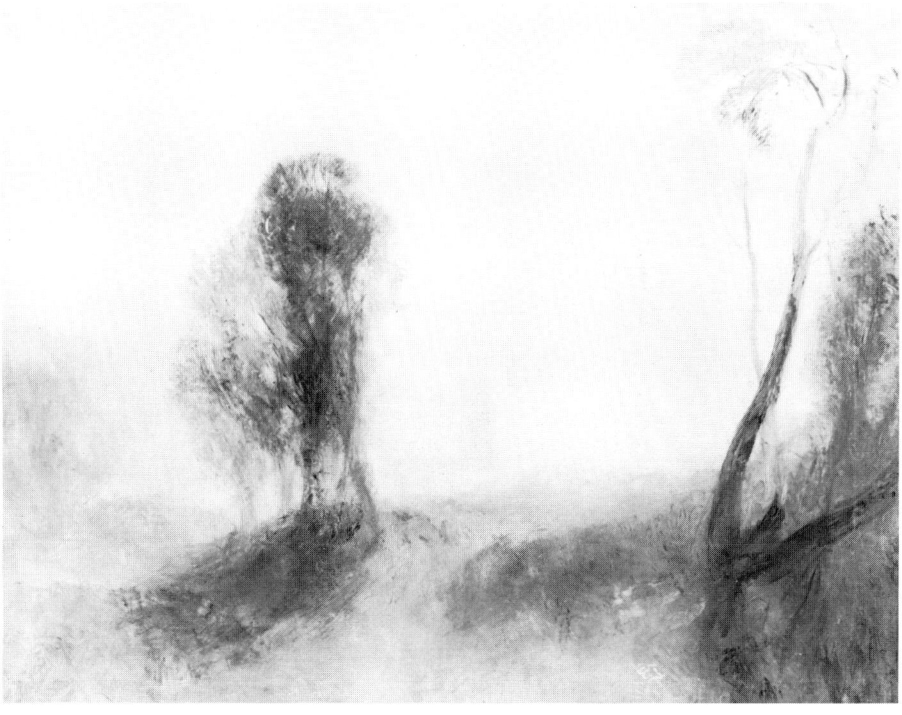

The painting called 'Sunrise, a Castle on a Bay': 'Solitude' in the Tate Gallery

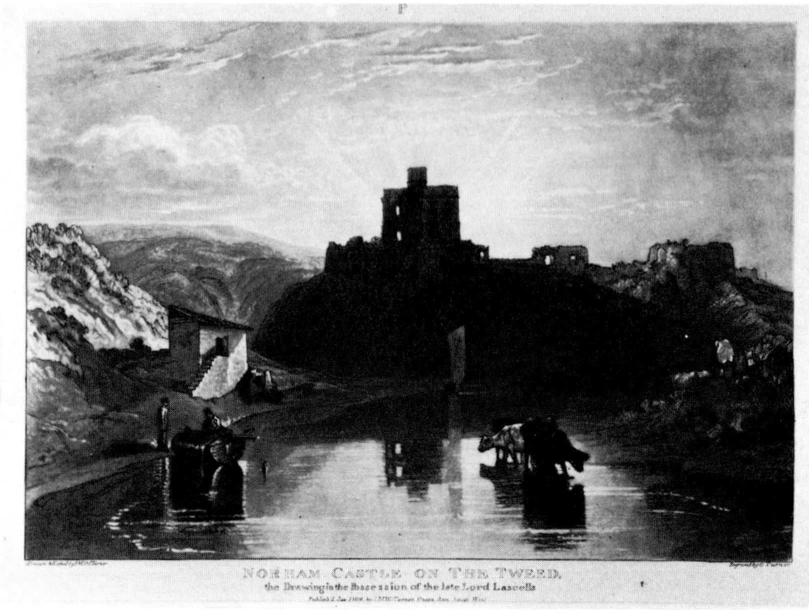

Plate 57 (P) *Norham Castle on the Tweed*

PART **12** 1 January 1816

The centre and the source

This part begins with one of Turner's most famous subjects. His first vision, in 1797, of Norham Castle stayed with him all his life, appearing in watercolours and engravings of all periods; and finally in the great chromatic painting, the original vision emptied of all but its purest elements, *Norham Castle, Sunrise* (1835–40). Cadell, the publisher who commissioned Turner to illustrate Sir Walter Scott, reported that the artist took off his hat when they passed the place; in fact he sketched the castle afresh for the Scott illustration, in the sketchbook CCLXVII.

The watercolour exhibited in 1798 was accompanied by a misquotation from Thomson's *Seasons*, which should read:

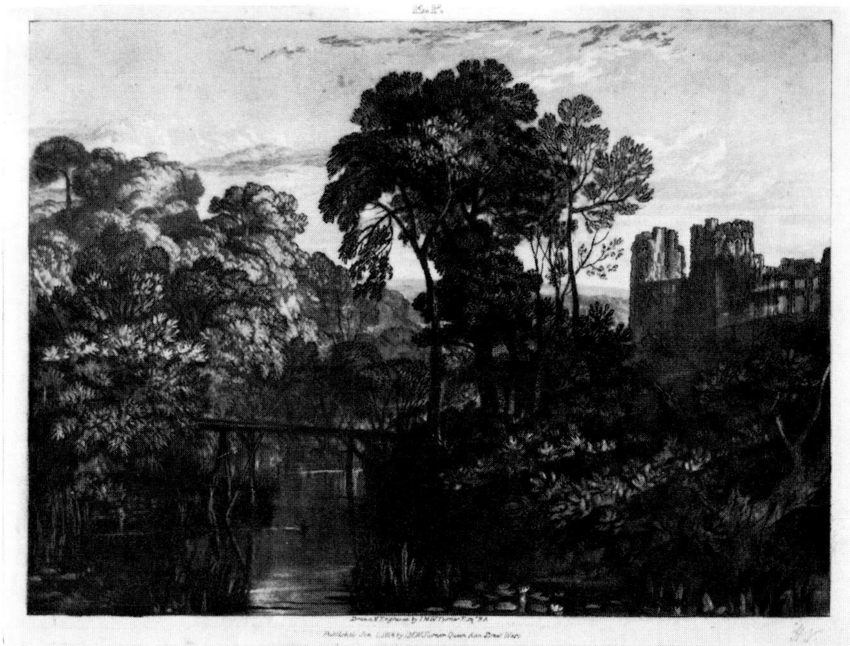

Plate 58 (EP) 'Berry Pomeroy Castle', sometimes called 'Raglan Castle'

But yonder comes the pow'rful king of day,
Rejoicing in the east. The less'ning cloud,
The kindling azure, and the mountain's brow
Illum'd with fluid gold, his near approach,
Betoken glad.

– rather a creaky sunrise – but the lines he chose tell us the sort of emotion which Turner, aged 22 and far from home, associated with this particular dawn, and never forgot. What he left out of the quotation was 'fluid gold' – perhaps to avoid criticism. He repaid the gold later in pigment, in the great oil painting.

In the *Liber* plate he exploits the inherent symmetry of the subject. He daringly moves the castle, just off-centre in the watercolour of 1798 (it is the one referred to in the title of the plate), to almost the dead centre of the plate. He makes his point, and demolishes a pious convention of his contemporaries, that nothing symmetrical can be picturesque.

One may also use the centre axis without placing the main subject there. In 'Berry Pomeroy Castle' a tree-trunk is placed exactly along the centre-line, the

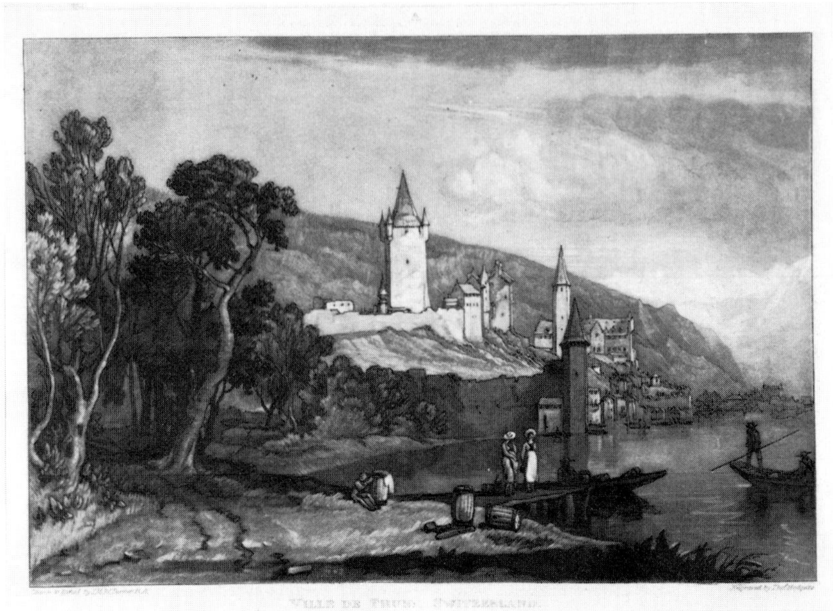

Plate 59 (A) *Ville de Thun – Switzerland*

most important elements of the composition being disposed to the left and downward, and to the right and upward, of the horizontal centre-line. The dead centre of the plate is picked out by a light gap in the foliage, and other lines of the compositon run through this point. A painting exhibited in Turner's gallery in 1812, of Ivybridge (12 miles towards Plymouth from Berry Pomeroy), also shows a very insistent use of the centre-line: the painting is divided into two halves, dark and light. It is cleverly done – never intrusive.

The working drawing for Berry Pomeroy, structured transparently in the sepia line and wash of the series, is one of the finest. But the line etching, which was probably by Dawe, certainly not by Turner, is lifeless and only saved by the master's control of tonal balance in the mezzotint. It works, but the atmosphere, the evanescence, and the Turnerian lost-and-found effect of the drawing are missing. Ruskin referred to this plate as 'Raglan'.

The tower of *Ville de Thun* is not centred exactly, though it appears to be because of the offsetting effect of the heavy, diagonal masses. In fact the centre of the plate falls on the base line of the tower at the foot of the right-hand buttress. The style of this plate is again quite different from that of the drawing, but this

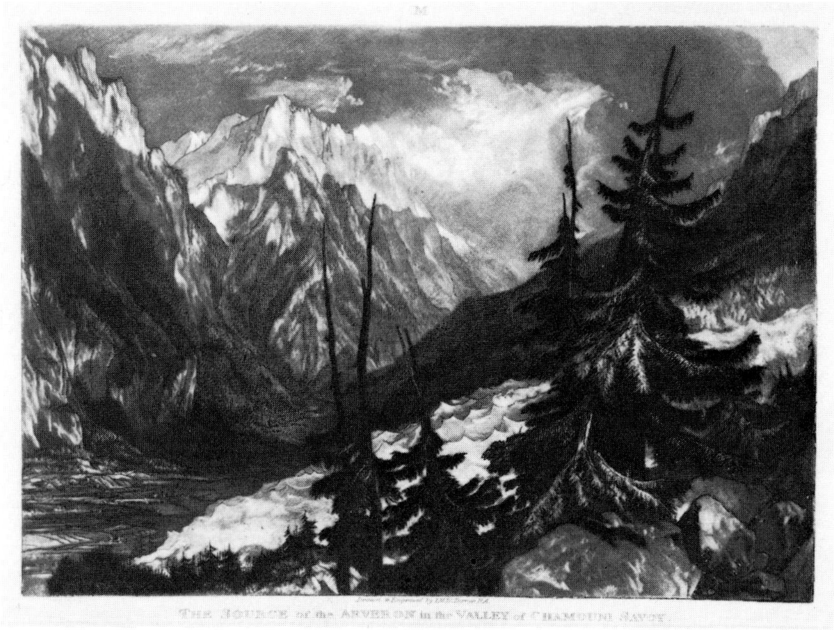

Plate 60 (M) *The Source of the Arveron in the Valley of Chamouni Savoy.* 3rd state

time with an improvement in effectiveness. Partly as a result of Turner's bold, etched line, but also because of a slightly formalised sense of 'colour' in Hodgetts' mezzotinting, it has a rich quality which looks forward to the later mezzotints of *Rivers of England* and to some of Turner's gouache drawings on the Meuse, in about 1826. It is a quality which gives *Ville de Thun* the texture of an early twentieth-century illustration to Grimm's *Fairy Tales* – one instance among many of Turner's originality in evolving new styles.

Another style, one identified by Ruskin, was the 'Alpine', embodied in the colour sketches of the large *St Gothard* sketchbook of 1802 and the drawings made from them for Walter Fawkes. One of the best known of these was adapted for the plate, *The Source of the Arveron.* 'Source' equals 'centre' perhaps: at the centre of this composition is an empty triangle, and the whole design is built of triangles. Turner himself was the engraver over a finicky etching, probably Dawe's according to Finberg, which fortunately disappears under the mezzotint.

The *Tenth Plague* . . . need I repeat the theme? Diagonals crossing at the centre are used to compart the composition, the architectural segment being particularly well handled by Turner and Say – smooth and dim in contrast to the shaggy,

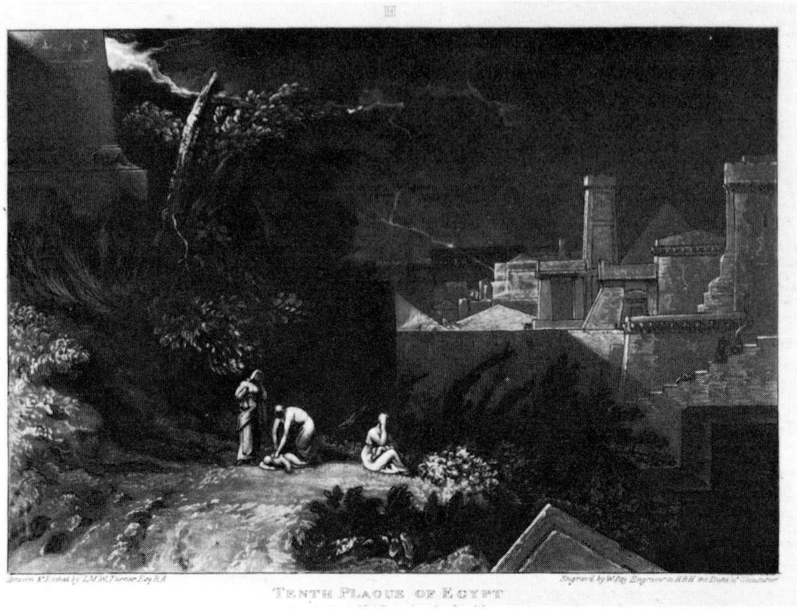

Plate 61 (H) *Tenth Plague of Egypt*

blasted shrubs and trees. The already strong geometry of the painting of 1802 is formalised and compressed in the plate.

There appears to be no ulterior theme linking the subjects in these centre-based compositions – or my divining powers have let me down. Perhaps the subjects themselves are so central to Turner's art that he disdained to provide a connection. More likely, he had run out of available plates. As it stands, the group of three castles, one Alpine landscape, and 'Slaying of the First-born', doesn't add up to any sort of unity. In *Norham Castle*, the first plate, we have the centrally placed sunrise as the source of life; in *Tenth Plague*, the last, death and darkness; but in between the message is not clear.

The 11th and 12th Parts were advertised in a part of W. B. Cooke's *Picturesque Views on the Southern Coast of England*, published 1816, with many line engravings after Turner. The advertisement stated that: 'the whole work will be comprised in twenty numbers, forming two volumes, ten numbers of which are published, containing fifty engravings . . . subscriptions received at Mr. Turner's, Queen Anne Street, Harley Street'.

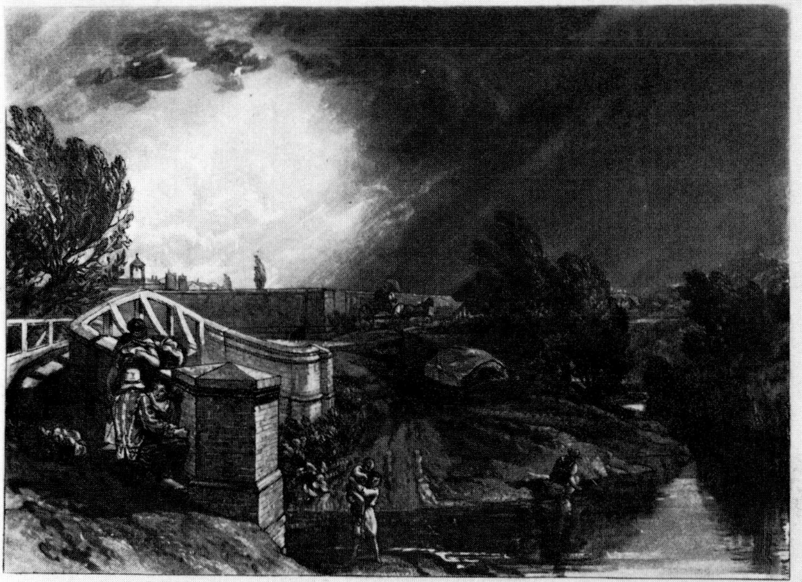

Plate 62 (P) *Watercress Gatherers, Rails Head Ferry Bridge, Twickenham.* A final trial proof

PART **13** 1 January 1819

Winds and weathers

Turner was very busy, particularly with topographical illustration commissions, and two years passed before he issued another part of *Liber Studiorum.* Though the impetus of the series may be fading, the vigour and inspiration of the plates is not less, and the high quality of the previous part is continued. He uses in this set a style of composition formed of triangular masses, well shown by the thrusting prow of the boat in *Inverary Castle.* In four of the plates he still keeps his eye on the dead centre: but he is now less concerned with the bones of construction, or of contention. This chapter celebrates some differing effects of weather – not, of course, that he has ignored the weather up to now, but here he shows how it may affect the whole scene and become the subject of the picture.

Starting with a squall in *Watercress Gatherers*, he turns what might sound like a scene of rustic peace into a moment of intense visual excitement. The design is

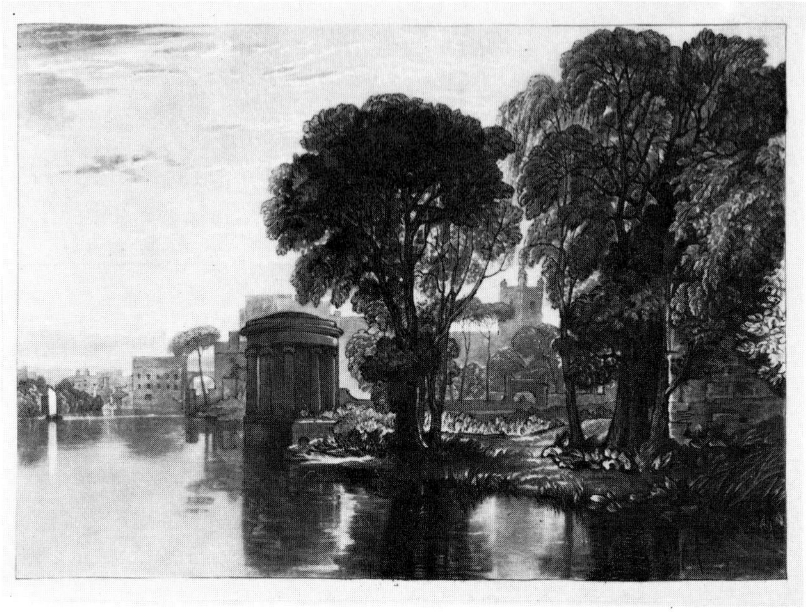

Plate 63 (EP) 'Isleworth'. A trial proof (b)

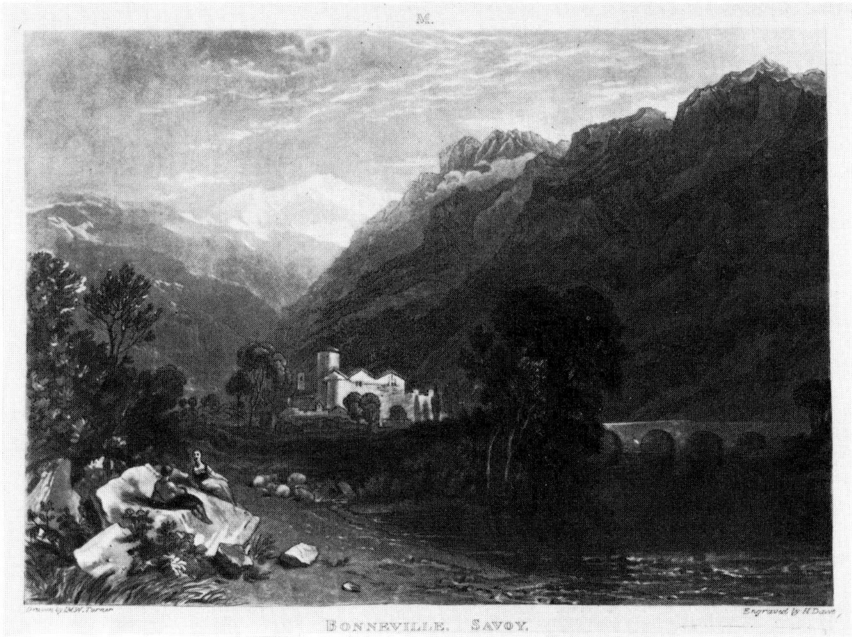

Plate 64 (M) *Bonneville, Savoy*. 2nd state

complex and surely one of his finest, even allowing for the figures which are ill-drawn.

'Isleworth' evokes a calm evening. The brightness of the sky spreads its influence throughout the picture by reflection in the motionless Thames and by delicately piercing the foliage of the trees. Zion Ferry House, where Turner had lived, may be the building at the extreme right, or behind that. A sepia pen and wash study in a sketchbook of 1807 (XCVII; see Wilkinson, 1974, p. 84) has a similar composition in reverse.

Bonneville is also calm, but it is the lazy stillness of a warm valley sheltered by high mountains. The couple basking on a rock have all the time in the world. Turner once again allows one of his best drawings to be interpreted by Dawe's unadventurous needle.

Wind is the active force in *Inverary Castle and Town* and everything in the picture expresses it. Even the distant hills have a cold, windy look, more so in the early proof (overleaf). Note Turner's modification of the crag above the town – still, even then, very emphatic compared with the accurate and beautiful pencil drawing of 1802. With *Aesacus and Hesperié* we are in the still depths of the woods, and the air is alive with sunlight. The line of the sun's rays and of a leaning trunk

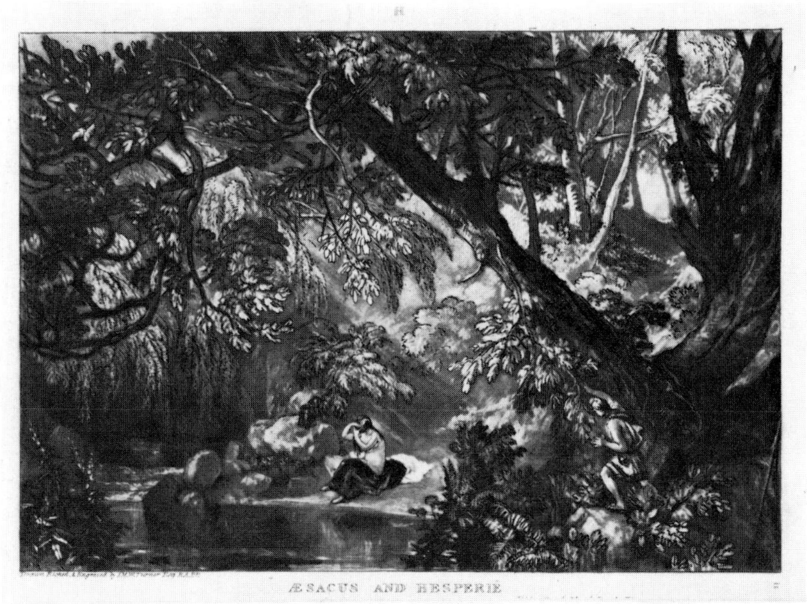

Plate 66 (H) *Aesacus and Hesperié. Vide Ovid Mets. Book XI.* 4th state

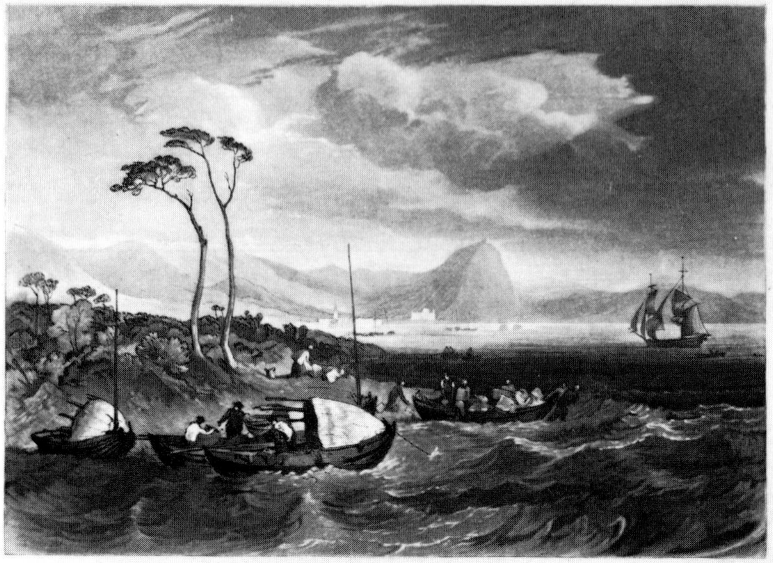

A trial proof (b) of Plate 65

Plate 65 (M) *Inverary Castle and Town, Scotland*

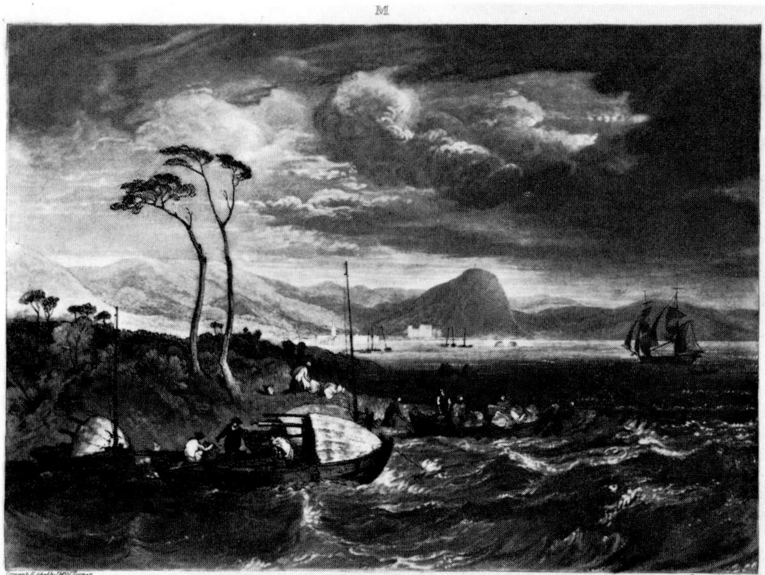

divides the picture into two large triangles crossed by the opposite diagonal of the rock formation, bearing out the geometrical theme of this group.

For once in the *Liber* a young girl appears. It is odd that Turner, who had two daughters, and was at great pains to introduce children into the early Pastoral plates, seems to concentrate on small boys. Perhaps at that stage he could identify more easily with them – and Sarah Danby's other children may have been boys of the right age to be models. He is supposed to have included his daughters in two major paintings: *Crossing the Brook* (1815) and *A Frosty Morning* (1813). The girl in *Watercress Gatherers* only makes her appearance after the etched stage; and Lupton, who considerably improved the other figures, may have had something to do with it. Lupton was very good: after six trial states, the plate then wore well and needed no reworking after publication.

Turner Bequest LVIII 9, 'Inverary Castle', 13 × 19¼ inches (33 × 49 cm).
Pencil, chalk, wash and white on paper tinted with brown

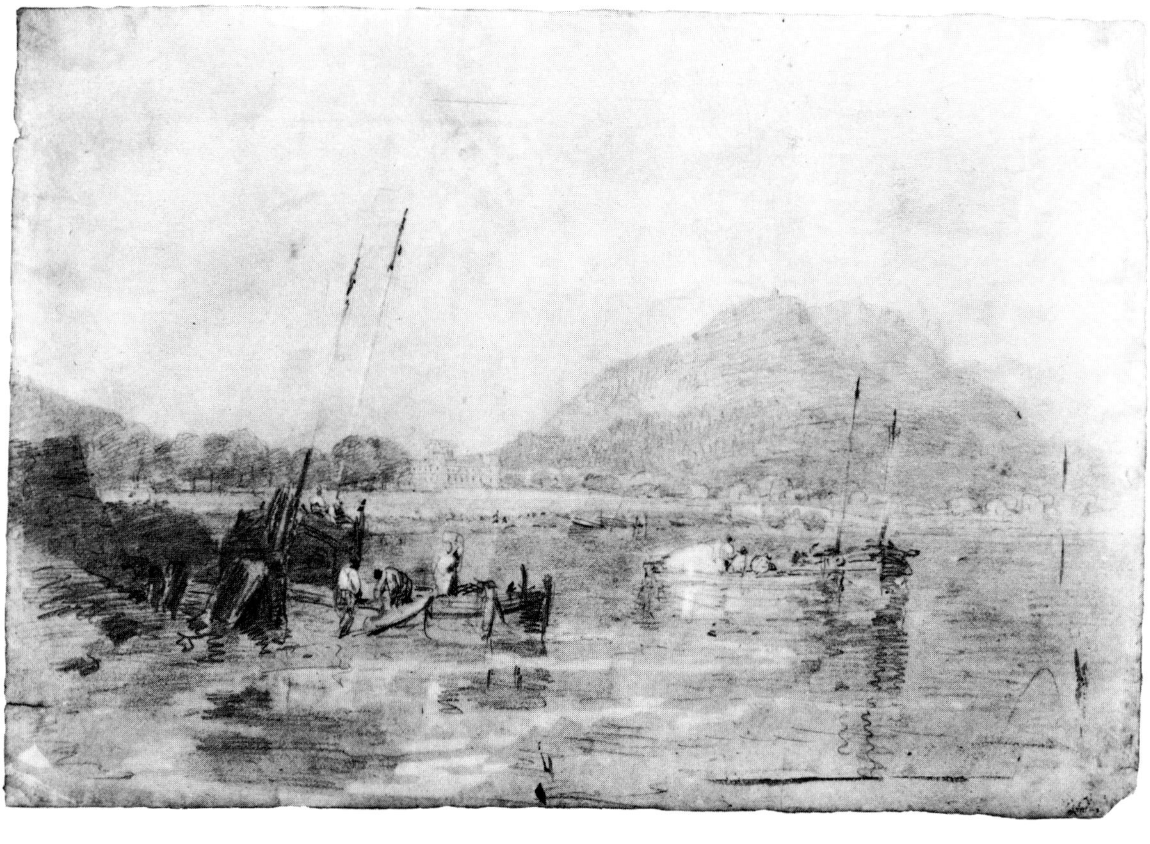

PART **14** 1 January 1819

Symphonic sketches

Parts 13 and 14 were the last to be published, both on the same day. In this part the theme is nothing analytical: it is the orchestration of the whole.

We have had:

1 bridges/connections
2 white accents/voids and solids
3 geometrical solids/lighting
4 movement within the picture
5 contrast
6 water/angles
7 symbolism, or sentiment
8 recession
9 movement out of the picture
10 land-use/scale
11 man in the landscape
12 balance about the centre
13 weather/triangles

Now we may expect to find several of these aspects of landscape combined in the five plates here. One feature provides a unifying touch – Turner's favourite round arch. Since completeness is the theme, he would include that.

East Gate, Winchelsea, with the other Winchelsea plate (Plate 42), was one of the first conceptions for the *Liber*, if we can believe the dating of the *Sussex* sketchbook, XCII.* Turner plays his centre-line trick again – but he has done this many times – see the 'Ships in a Breeze' (Plate 10) for a glaring example of actual, rather than pretended, centring. The atmosphere of *East Gate* is benign – truly pastoral. All the aspects of landscape mentioned above appear, except water – and even that is hinted at by the ferns and docks in the foreground. (Leaves of the giant dock, the dominant ground plant of the *Liber*, even appear in the Egyptian sand of Plate 6.)

East Gate, Winchelsea is a very satisfying picture. We may note particularly the

*See Wilkinson, 1974, pp. 70–1, for reproductions.

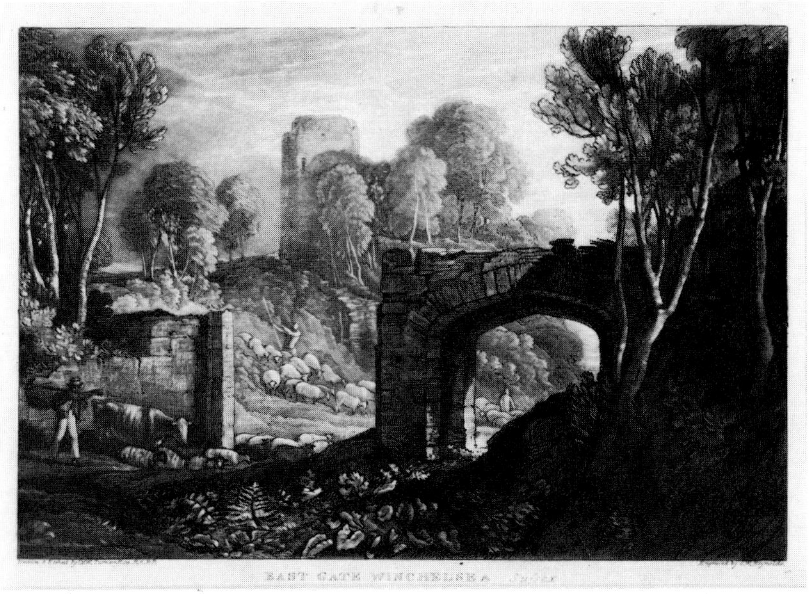

Plate 67 (P) *East Gate, Winchelsea, Sussex*. 3rd state

movement of converging lines, balanced by the subtler movements of the sky beyond the tower. Reynolds' engraving quite misrepresents the grainy, lichenous quality of the drawing; but it hangs together well.

Isis, by contrast, is strange and emblematic, perhaps of the classical qualities which Turner had sought in his work, and found along the middle reaches of the Thames. *Dido and Aeneas* and other classical compositions were, on the evidence of the sketchbooks, conceived on the Thames. There is a pen and wash version of *Dido* with Thameside willows.* Finberg describes *Isis* as a *capriccio*; but the tempo is *larghetto*. The subject is in fact a classical folly by the lake at Petworth House, with Windsor Castle and the Thames appearing in the distance, so that we are presented with a montage of two scenes, both important to Turner.

In *Ben Arthur* the thematic arch is inverted: a simple composition but very lively in handling. So lively were the first trials that a considerable amount of toning down had to be done. Lupton again shows his fine sense of balance.

Interior of a Church, entirely worked by Turner, contains, Ruskin informs us, his only drawing of a clergyman. This plate, in a series of landscapes, is quite out of place – perhaps a symptom of the author's failing enthusiasm? But he needed

*See Wilkinson, 1977, pp. 120–2 (or Wilkinson, 1974, pp. 106–9).

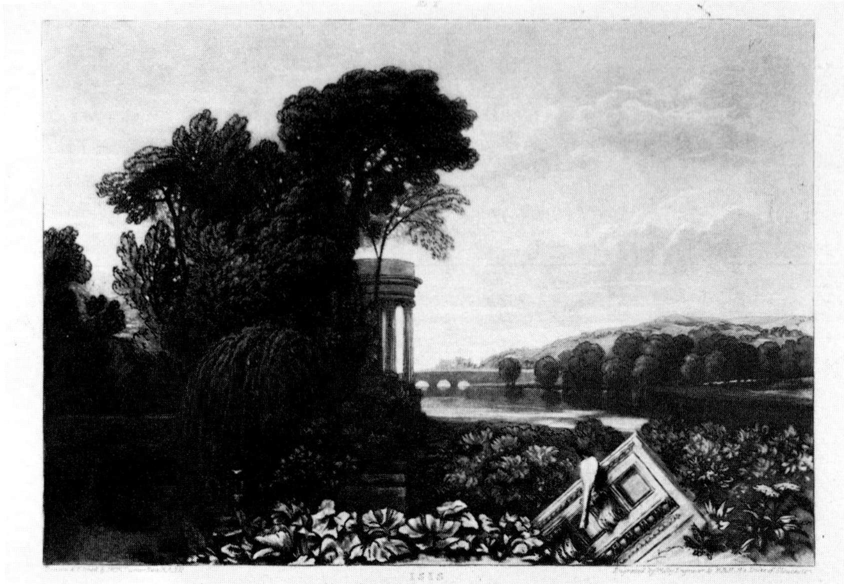

Plate 68 (EP) *Isis*

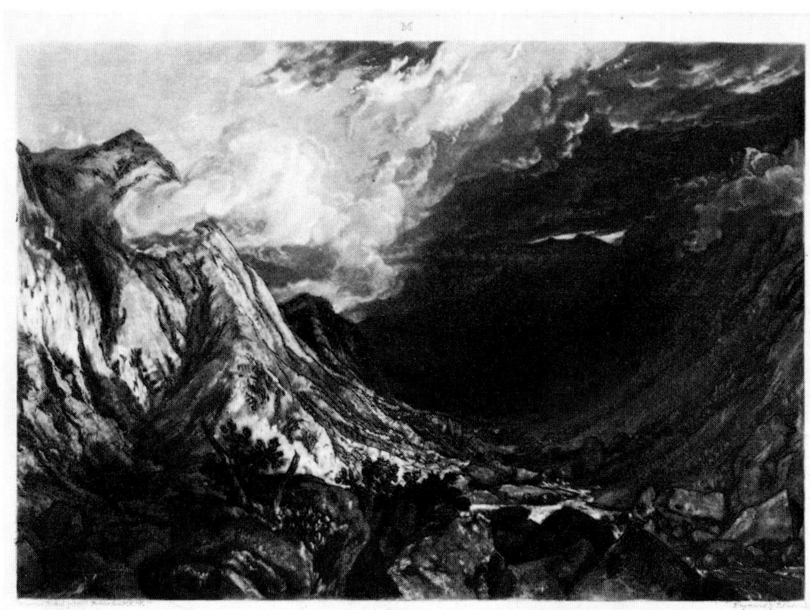

Plate 69 (M) *Ben Arthur, Scotland*

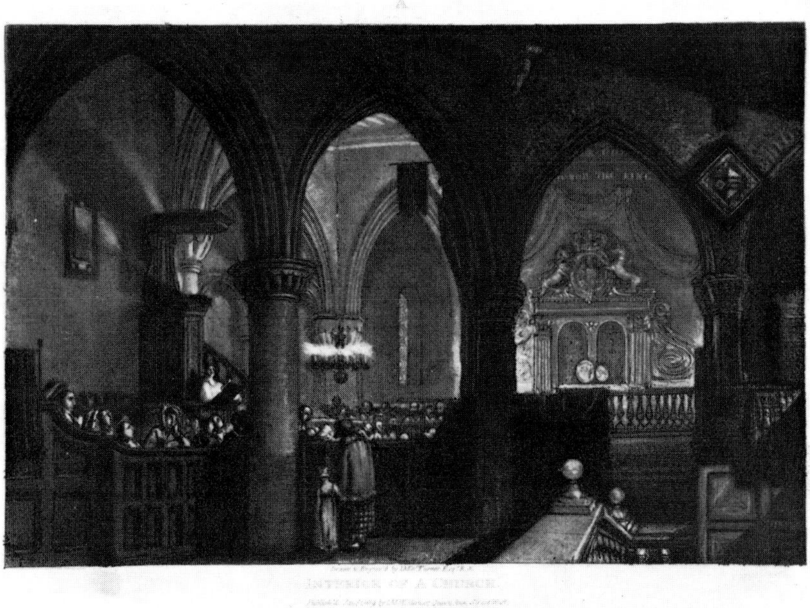

Plate 70 (A) *Interior of a Church*

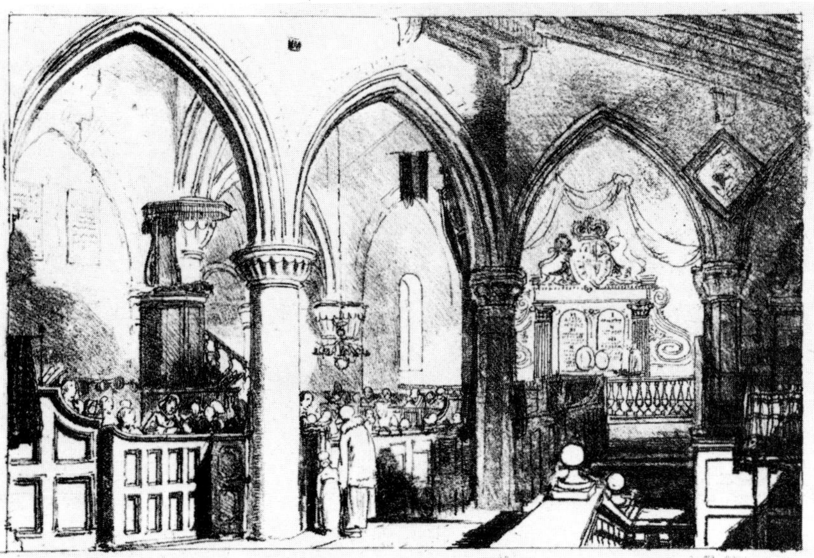

Turner's etching in soft ground. Pantzer collection, Indianapolis

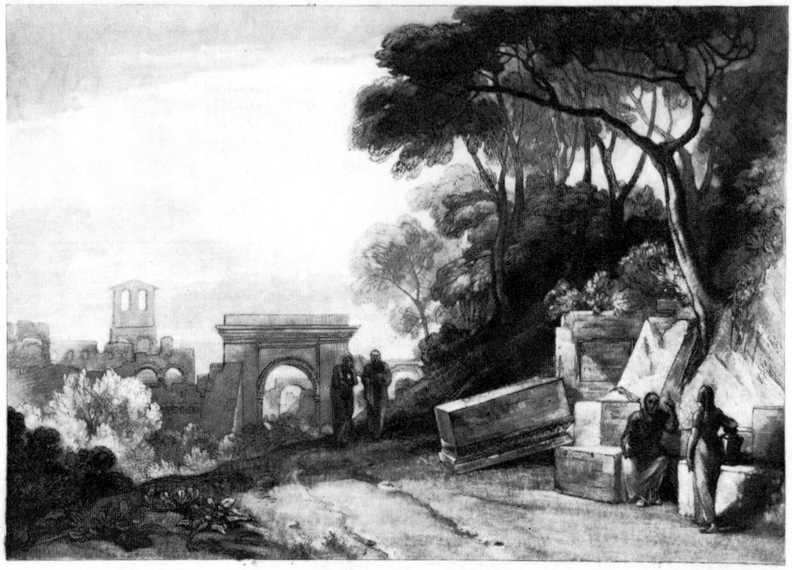

Plate 71 (H) *Christ and the Woman of Samaria*. A trial proof

some Gothic arches. The composition is skilful, complex and satisfying. The little, round-arched window is pinned to the centre of the plate; the lighter column is at a Golden Section. All the lessons of landscape that can be applied are certainly well orchestrated here. Early proof states show a 'daylight' effect which was toned down to the rather low-key effect of the published states, with candles burning.

The last published plate is *Christ and the Woman of Samaria*. Turner illustrated a few New Testament subjects in his paintings, but the painting with a similar title* is quite different in design. In this plate he employs, without show, at least a dozen of his elements of landscape, including a figure at the measured centre and a nice pattern of receding arches at a Golden Section. Water, his favourite theme, is only implied: 'Whosoever drinketh of the water I shall give him shall never thirst.' Two other well-known quotations occur in the story: 'One soweth, and another reapeth'; and 'A prophet hath no honour in his own country' – a truth that Turner, even by 1819, had both proved and disproved.

*Tate Gallery, no. 1875.

THE ENGRAVERS OF *LIBER STUDIORUM*

Plate	*Etcher*	*Engraver*
2 to 21	J. M. W. Turner	Charles Turner
22	J. M. W. Turner	William Say
23	J. M. W. Turner	Robert Dunkarton
24	J. M. W. Turner	William Say
25	J. M. W. Turner	Robert Dunkarton
26	J. M. W. Turner	Charles Turner
27	J. M. W. Turner	William Say
28	J. M. W. Turner	J. M. W. Turner
29	J. M. W. Turner	William Say
30	J. M. W. Turner	William Say
31	J. M. W. Turner	Thomas Hodgetts
32	J. M. W. Turner	Robert Dunkarton
33	J. M. W. Turner	J. C. Easling
34	J. M. W. Turner	William Say
35	J. M. W. Turner	J. M. W. Turner
36	J. M. W. Turner	Thomas Hodgetts
37	J. M. W. Turner	Robert Dunkarton
38	J. M. W. Turner	William Say
39	J. M. W. Turner	J. M. W. Turner
40	J. M. W. Turner	W. Armis and J. C. Easling
41	J. M. W. Turner	George Clint
42	J. M. W. Turner	J. C. Easling
43	J. M. W. Turner	F. C. Lewis
44	J. M. W. Turner	J. M. W. Turner
45	J. M. W. Turner	George Clint
46	J. M. W. Turner	Robert Dunkarton
47	J. M. W. Turner	J. C. Easling
48	J. M. W. Turner	W. Armis
49	J. M. W. Turner	William Say
50	J. M. W. Turner	J. M. W. Turner
51	J. M. W. Turner	Henry Dawe
52	J. M. W. Turner	Thomas Lupton

53	J. M. W. Turner	William Say
54	probably Henry Dawe	Henry Dawe
55	J. M. W. Turner	J. M. W. Turner
56	J. M. W. Turner	Thomas Lupton
57	J. M. W. Turner	Charles Turner
58	probably Henry Dawe	J. M. W. Turner
59	J. M. W. Turner	Thomas Hodgetts
60	probably Henry Dawe	J. M. W. Turner
61	J. M. W. Turner	William Say
62	J. M. W. Turner	Thomas Lupton
63	J. M. W. Turner	Henry Dawe
64	Henry Dawe?	Henry Dawe
65	J. M. W. Turner	Charles Turner
66	J. M. W. Turner	J. M. W. Turner
67	J. M. W. Turner	Samuel Reynolds
68	J. M. W. Turner	William Say
69	J. M. W. Turner	Thomas Lupton
70	J. M. W. Turner	J. M. W. Turner
71	J. M. W. Turner	Samuel Reynolds

The plates were printed by S. Lahee

The unpublished plates

The published *Liber Studiorum* was brought to a premature, but, thanks to Turner's professionalism, a satisfactory conclusion. The unpublished plates are witness to his intentions for a more impressive finale. Perhaps the 'orchestration' theme was to continue, with the engraving medium gradually emerging as creative, not merely reproductive. But this would have devalued the earlier plates: a good reason for calling a halt!

While he experimented with pure mezzotint – rarely, it seems, able to satisfy himself – he was producing watercolours finished and expressly designed for line engraving and mezzotint. These worked very well. He and his engravers understood and respected each other (though Turner was frequently rude: when he couldn't be autographic he was autocratic).

He eventually gave up the idea of engraving as an expressive medium. We do not know at what stage the plate numbered 91 was done, only that it was based on a small painting of 1809. I would have thought that it indicated a breakthrough. It looks back to both Gainsborough and Goya. Only genius could have joined *these* two lines, and the conjunction was more promising, surely, than a marriage of Claude and Wilkie. But it may be that the effects of Plate 91 seemed too easy. The whole thing was a sketch (the painting had been so titled), and not, by the standards of the day, important. The autographic mezzotints, here and in the 'Little Liber', all show signs of struggle and dissatisfaction. Of the remaining plates more or less in the *Liber* convention, 'Sheepwashing' and 'Crowhurst' are inspiring; the rest, by comparison, dull and repetitive.

The way forward was through colour. In illustration, too, it was the way to stretch his engraver's skill. After the *Liber*, everything he put before the engravers was, uncompromisingly, in colour. Not quite uncompromising though, for the palette was peculiar, and deliberately so. But that is another story.

Finberg lists number 72 to 91, stopping short of Rawlinson's 92 to 100 (later modified to 99), which exist only as drawings.

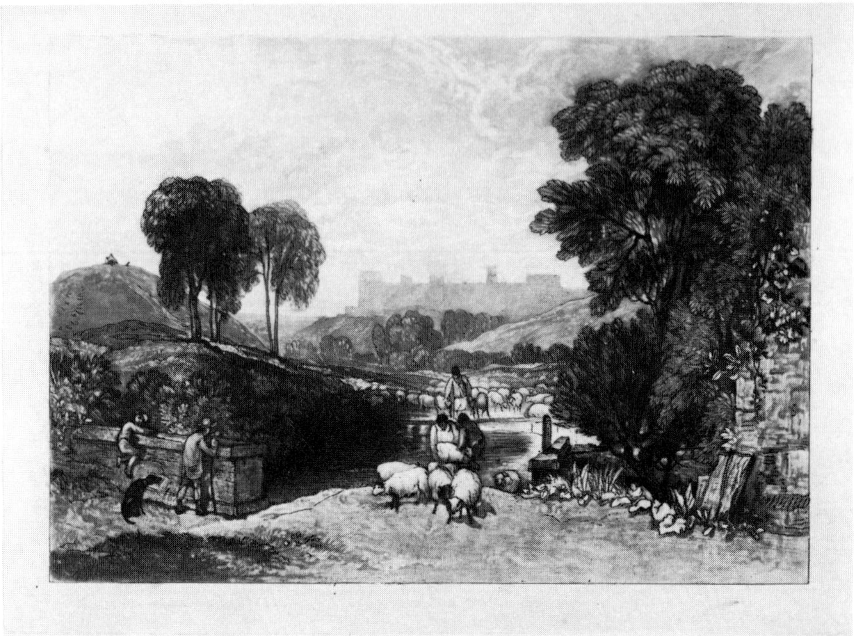

Sheepwashing, Windsor. Etched by Turner, engraved by Charles Turner

F72 Apuleia in Search of Apuleius*
F73 Glaucus and Scylla*
F74 Windsor Castle from Salt Hill or Sheepwashing, Windsor
F75 Dumbarton Rock
F76 Crowhurst
F77 The Temple of Jupiter in the Island of Aegina*
F78 Via Mala*
F79 Ploughing, Eton
F80 Pan and Syrinx*
F81 Stonehenge at Daybreak
F82 The Felucca*
F83 The Stork and Aqueduct
F84 The Lost Sailor
F85 Moonlight at Sea
F86 Moonlight on the Medway
F87 Kingston Bank
F88 The Deluge*
F89 Flounder Fishing, Battersea*
F90 Narcissus and Echo
F91 Sand Bank with Gipsies

*not illustrated.

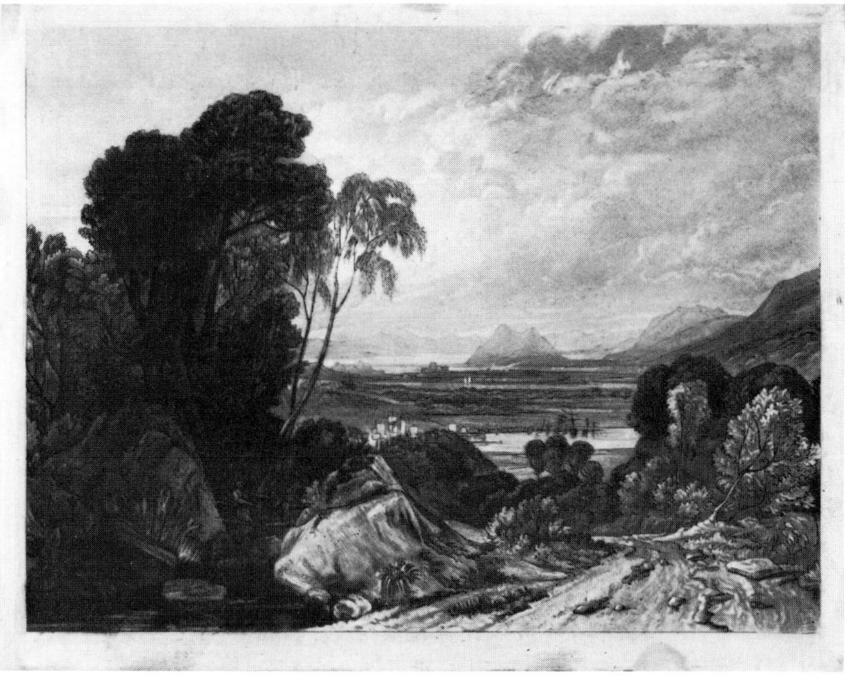

Dumbarton Rock. Etched by ?, engraved by Lupton

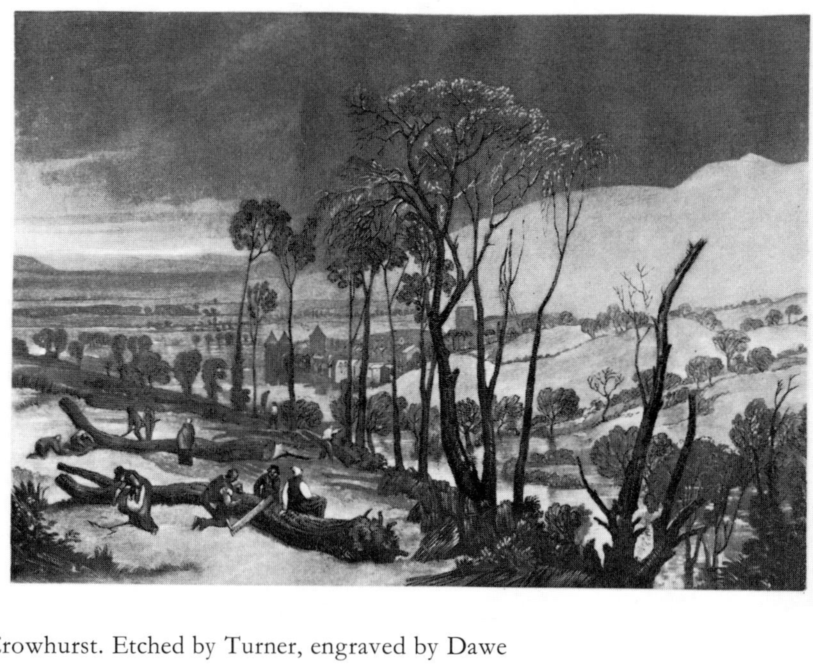

Crowhurst. Etched by Turner, engraved by Dawe

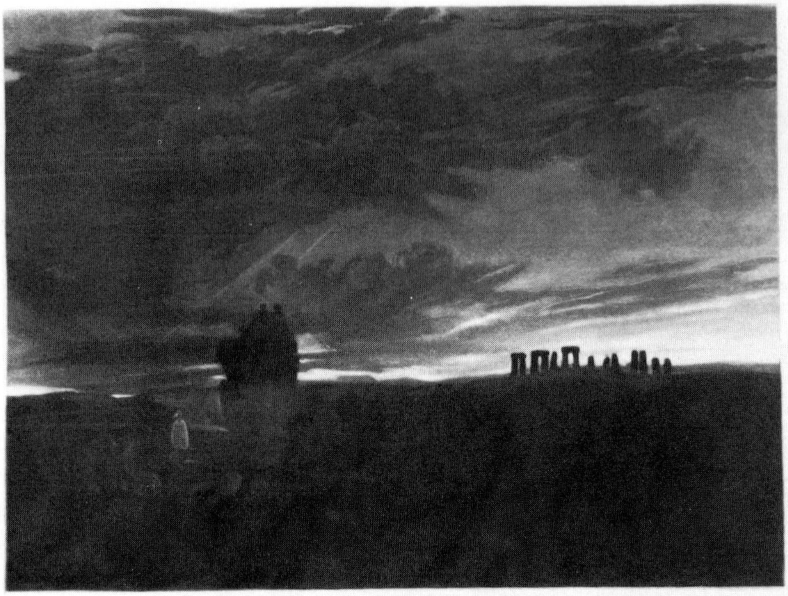

Stonehenge at Daybreak. Mezzotint almost certainly by Turner

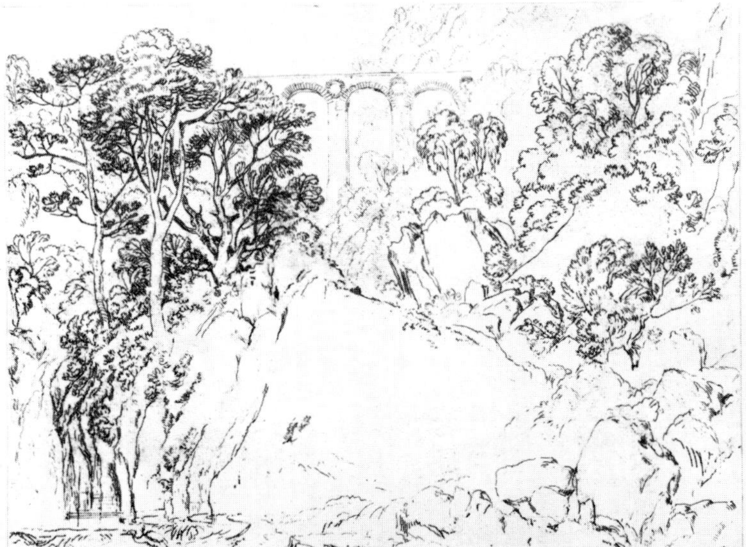

Stork and Aqueduct, or Heron's Pool. Turner's etching

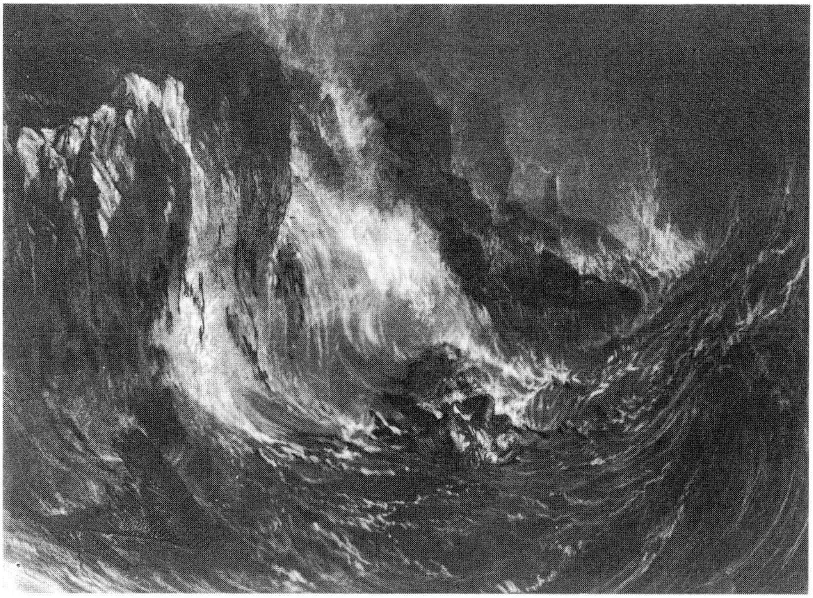

The Lost Sailor. Aquatint and mezzotint by Turner. Bullard Collection, Boston

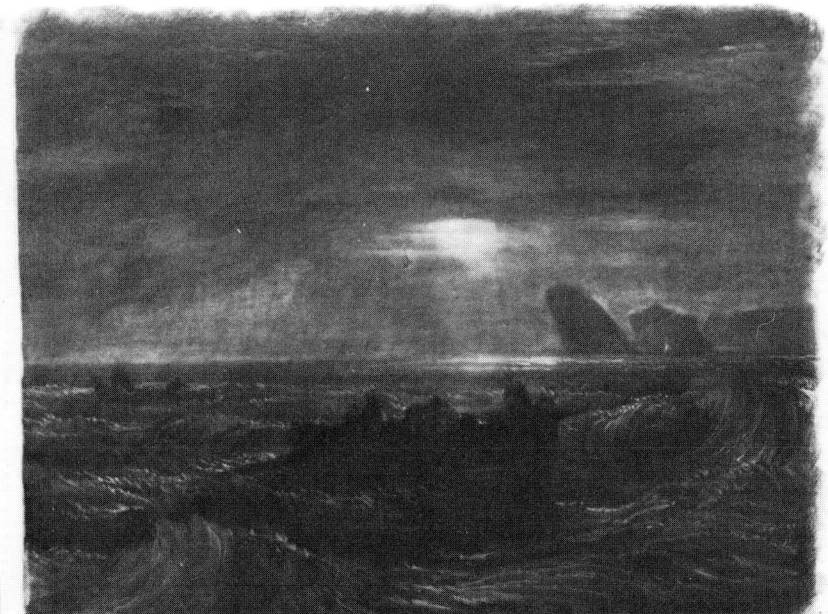

Moonlight at Sea. Mezzotint by Turner, one of two proofs known

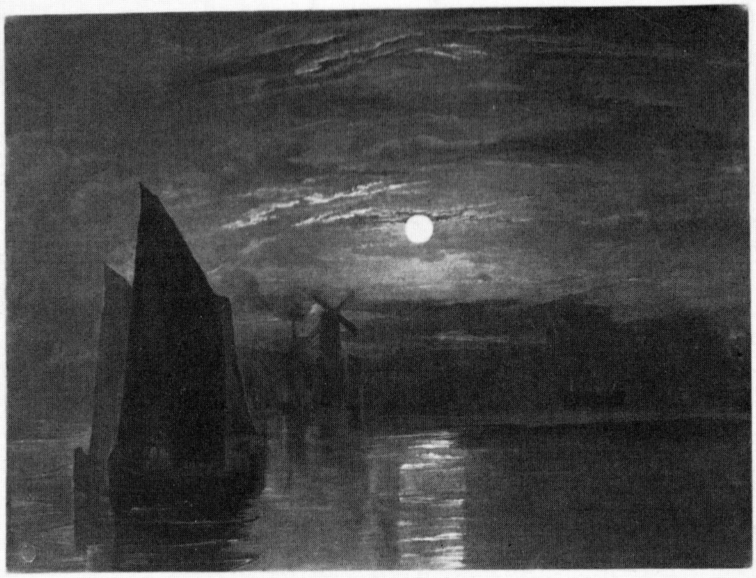

Moonlight on the Medway. 3rd state of a mezzotint (by Dawe?)

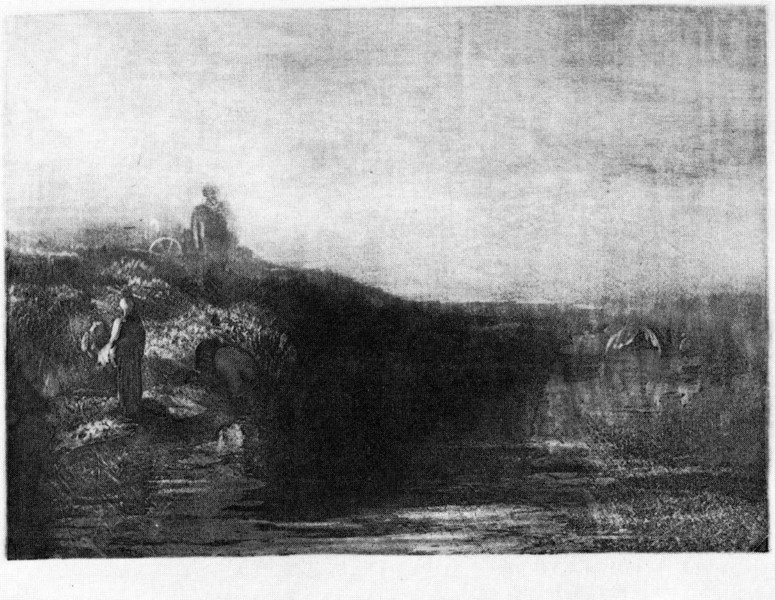

Kingston Bank. Mezzotint by Turner, proofed after his death

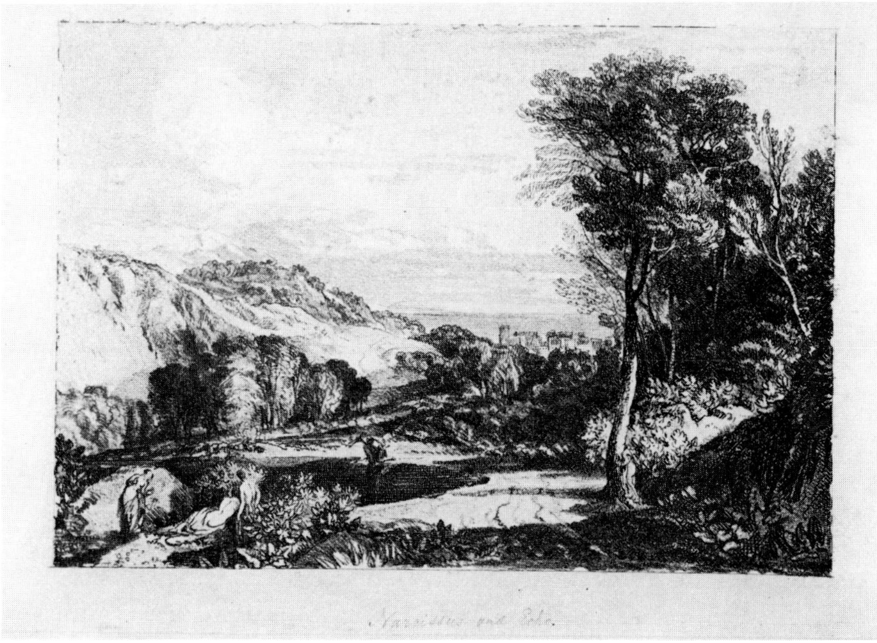

Narcissus and Echo. Soft ground etching by Turner after his painting of 1804

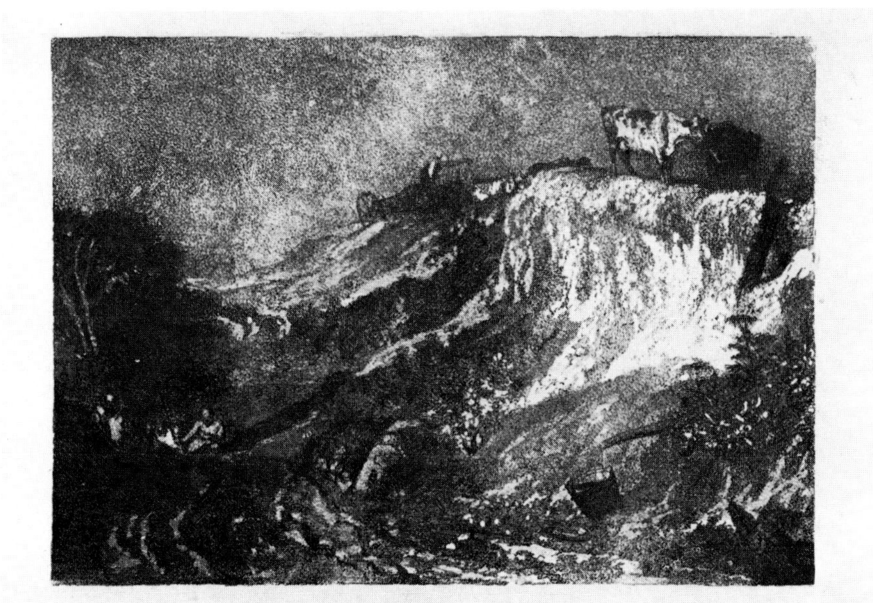

Sandbank with Gypsies, 2nd state – the only proof

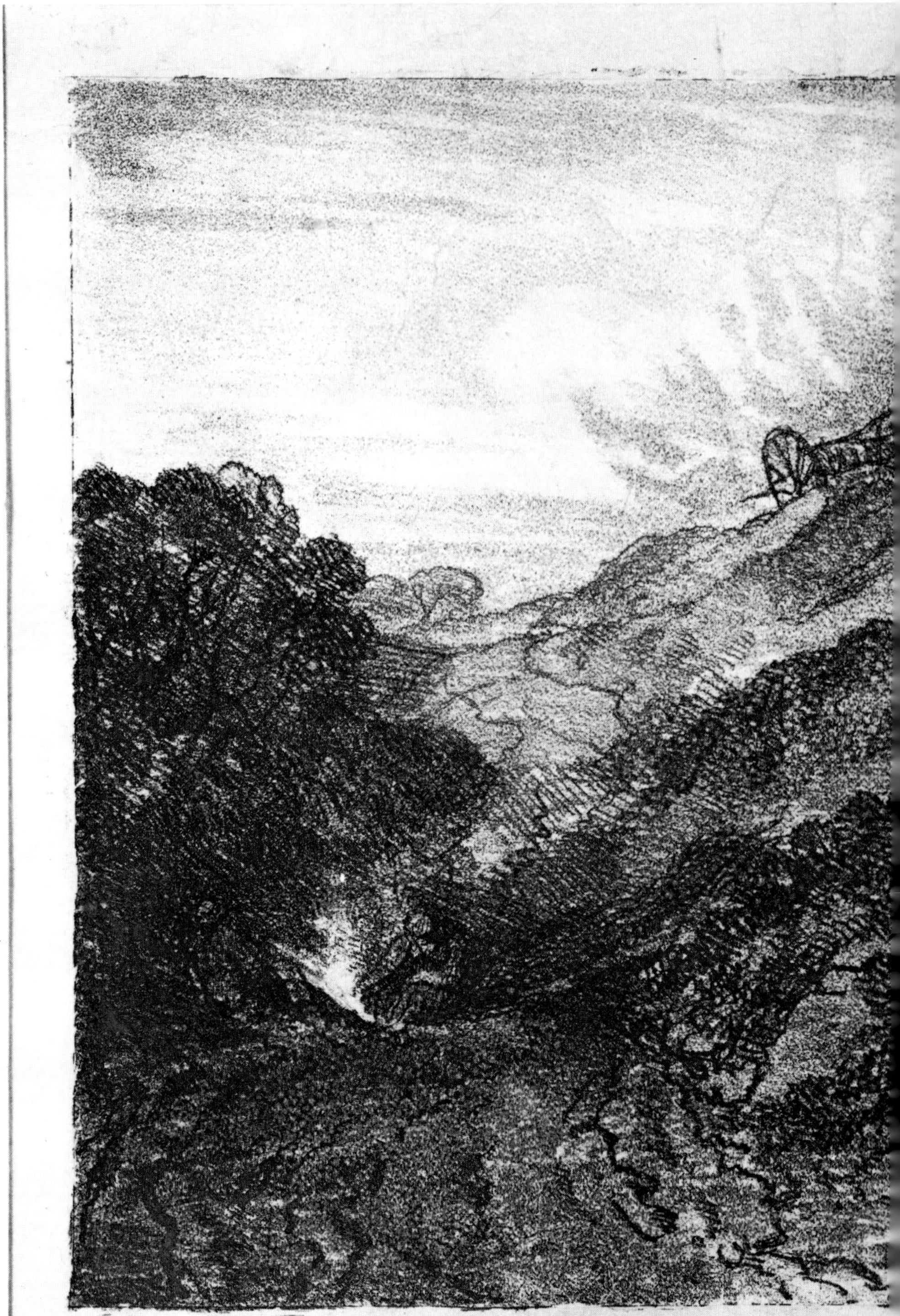

Sandbank with Gypsies, 1st state. One of two proofs known. Actual size

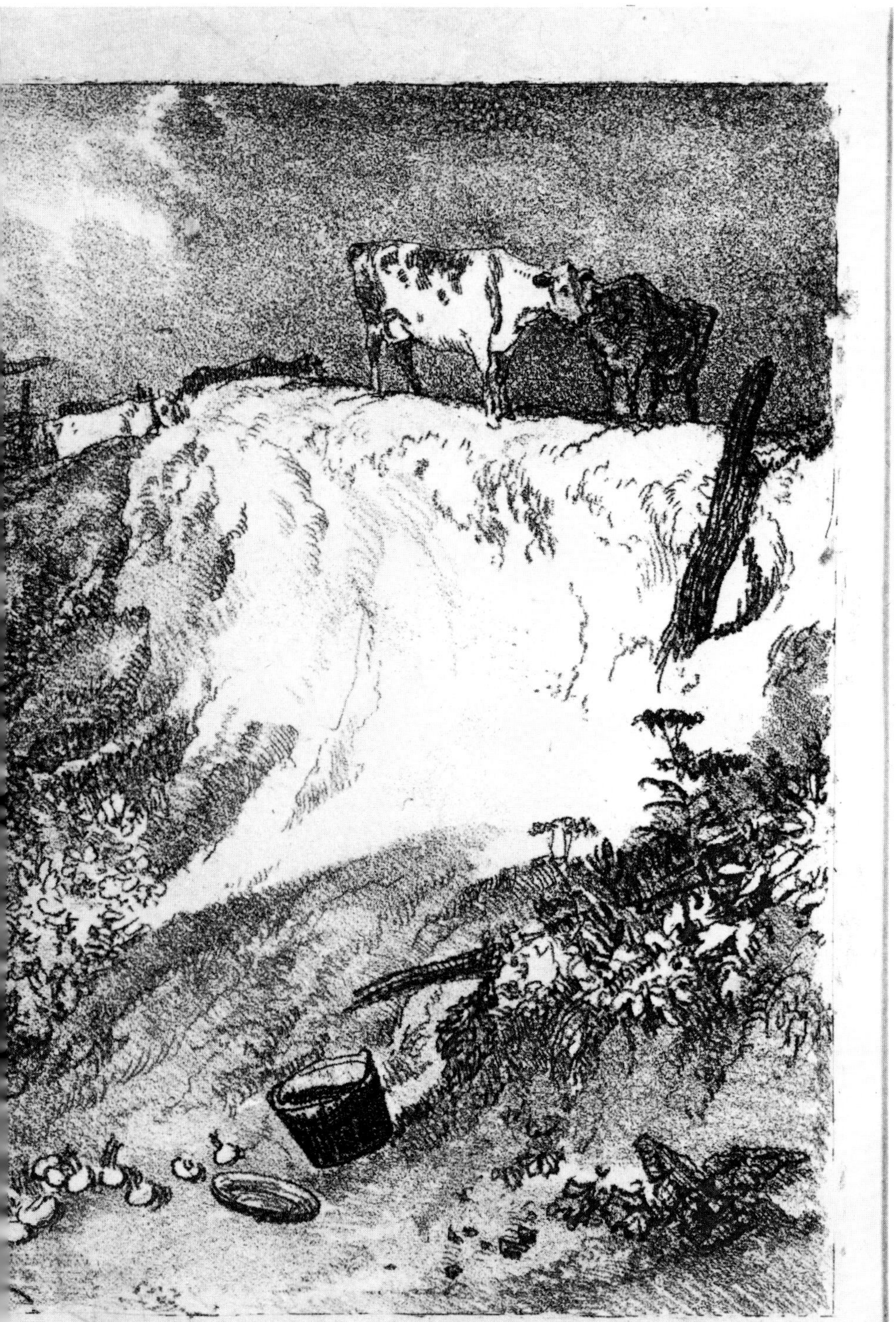
ws on a hill –

APPENDIX: TURNER AND THE GOLDEN SECTION

A line or a rectangle divided in the ratio of 1 : 1.61805398 . . . is said to be divided at a Golden Section. It is golden in the alchemist's sense, of a magic formula. If *a* is the smaller part and *b* the larger,

$$a : b :: b : (a+b)$$

and so you can continue dividing up your rectangle, or picture, in classical proportions; classical, because the formula has been known and used since Hellenic times. It was part of the mystique of the Pythagorans and it is easy to see why, once you begin to investigate its implications.

The nearest rational numbers for *a* and *b* are 8 and 13. These are part of the series 1, 1, 2, 3, 5, 8, 13, 21, 34, 55, 89, 144, 233, etc. (each number being the sum of the previous two), called the Fibonacci series, after Filius Bonacci who rediscovered it in the early Renaissance. The Fibonacci series has some surprising echoes in the natural world. A hive of bees multiplies precisely and inevitably according to the series. Species of many-petalled flowers conform, and so do fir cones, with, say, 8 spirals left and 13 right. Quite humble weeds branch and flower according to the early numbers in the series. It has a harmonic basis in musical scales. Its Pythagorean applications produce a logarithmic spiral (snail shell) based on

$$\frac{a}{b} = \frac{b}{(a+b)}$$

and the mystical figure, the pentagon: for *a* is the side of a pentagon of which *b* is the diagonal. Completing the diagonals produces a five-pointed star, each of the triangles of which has its sides in the Golden Ratio. The whole construction is full of intriguing resonances – but irrelevant to our subject.

To construct a Golden Section of a given line AB,
draw BC, half AB, at right angles.
With radius CB cut CA at X.
With radius AX cut AB at ϕ,
the Golden Section.

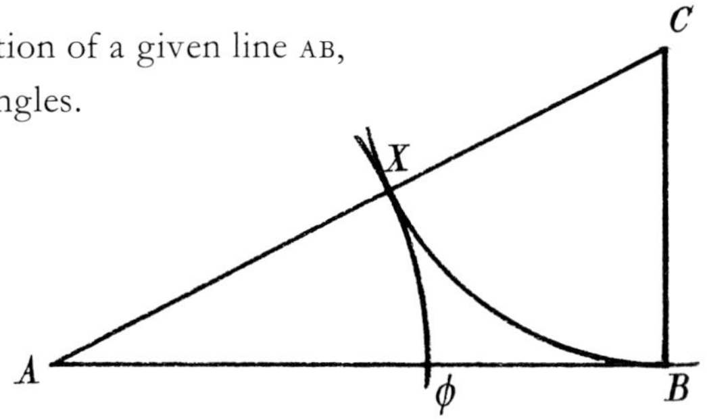

Artists and designers have used this and many other formulae and rules, for instance divisions into 3, 4, 5. Poussin, one of Turner's acknowledged masters, used the proportion 9:16 and is also said to have belonged to the Rosicrucians, who were keen on cabbalistic diagrams. Renaissance pictures and buildings can frequently be found to contain circles, various curves, diagonals, groups of converging lines, stars, octagons, triangles and pentagons. There was some reaction to all this geometry in philosophical and academic circles of the eighteenth century, early expressed in landscape gardening and later in Burke's *Sublime and Beautiful* (1756). Turner's youthful acquaintance with Richard Payne Knight and his collaboration with Sawrey Gilpin are enough to connect him with the theorists of the Picturesque who were essentially opposed to geometrical formulae. But he was only partly a product of the Picturesque: he was a good Academician first and last. Du Fresnoy's rules were articles of faith, actually printed and bound with Reynolds' *Discourses*. The *De Arte Graphica* of du Fresnoy refers to colour, but at least assures us that rules and theories were respected, though used, according to Reynolds' advice, with restraint: 'Practice must in some cases precede theory.'

Turner's Diploma picture, *Dolbadarn Castle*, anyway, demonstrates his awareness of the Golden Section, uncompromisingly using both vertical and horizontal Golden Sections to place the castle itself. In the *Liber* he uses the ratio insistently in many plates and ignores it altogether in others. This is some indication, in a series intended to demonstrate the art of composition, of the value he set upon this particular formula.

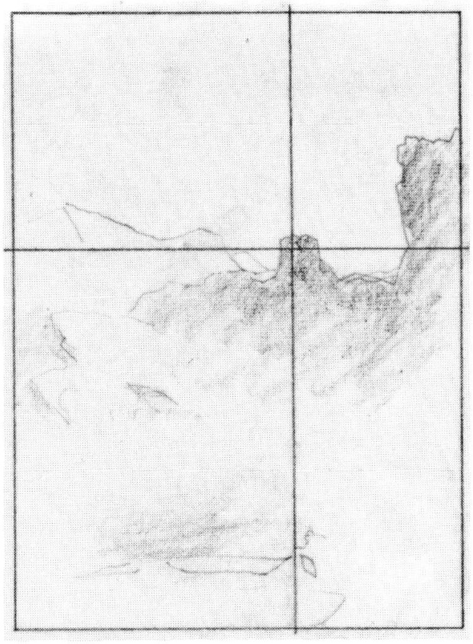

He was also fascinated by the centre-line, like della Francesca before him and Seurat after. Dividing the picture into two halves is a calamity warned against by most theorists of composition. Even architects, who up to the present century have always relied heavily on symmetry, avoid the error of the 'uninformed duality'. Part 12 of the *Liber* shows Turner playing very deliberately with the centre, centre-lines and diagonals, and achieving harmonious proportions in spite of a cardinal rule of both the Academic and the Picturesque schools.

Reviewing Turner's paintings generally, it becomes clear that he used the Golden Section very consistently in most of his important early works. In *Sun Rising through Vapour* (National Gallery) he uses the centre, and even more compelling, divides the resulting two halves for the placing of the various boats. Again dividing one of the vertical quarters, he places the sun itself very close to vertical and horizontal Golden Sections. The arc of the sun's path through the sky returns us to the centre-line of the picture.

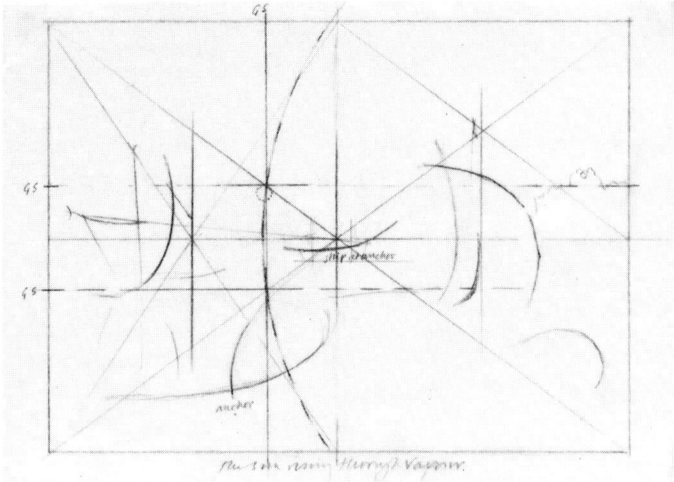

A similarly elaborate and static composition, the famous *Dort*, is very subtly divided, vertically and horizontally, into Golden Sections and secondary Golden Sections all arising from the rudder and mainsail of the nearest boat – the 'packet boat becalmed' – so that the whole picture is held in a mesh of 2, 3, 5, 8 proportions. The *Liber* Plate 44 is constructed in the same way, with secondary and tertiary Golden Sections, and it was clearly one of the origins of the *Dort* composition.

In later works such as *Norham Castle* (*c.* 1845), in fact one of several 'revisions' of *Liber* plates, the Golden Section appears again, with the centre-line. Sometimes, as in *The Fighting Temeraire*, *Rain, Steam and Speed* and *Snowstorm at Sea*, apparent movement is achieved by placing important elements just before or just after they might be expected to strike the Golden Section. Such subtle mechanics are typical of Turner, who had every device at his fingertips, and, like a great concert pianist, was always 'in practice'.

It is often remarked of the Golden Section that it can be found in most works of art once you start looking. This is true, and we must conclude that, like the rest of the import of my remarks on the *Liber*, it is all speculation and nothing is proved according to the tenets of modern art-scholarship. You, the reader, must decide whether such speculations are idle and unproductive.

This diagram can be traced and applied to the reproductions in this book

PICTORIAL INDEX OF THE PUBLISHED PLATES OF *LIBER STUDIORUM*

Part

1

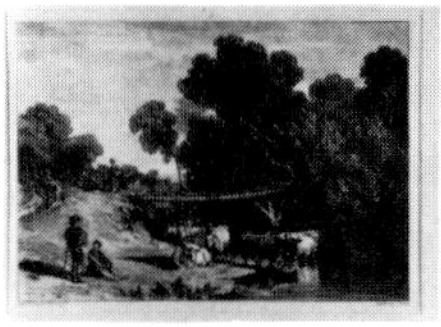
2 Bridge and Cows

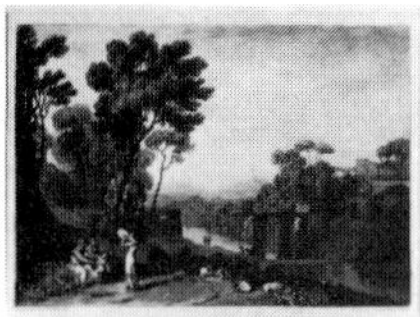
3 Woman with Tambourine

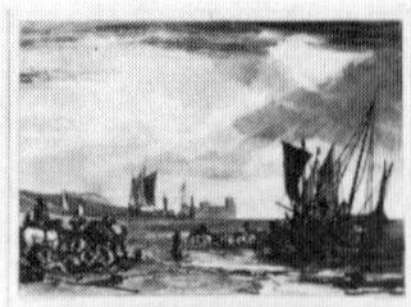
4 Flint Castle

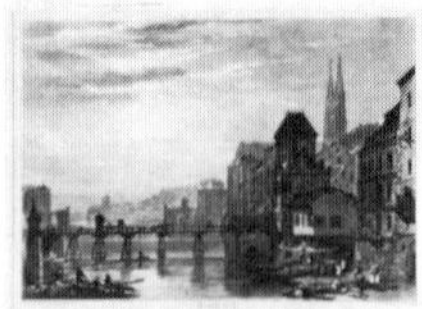
5 *Basle*

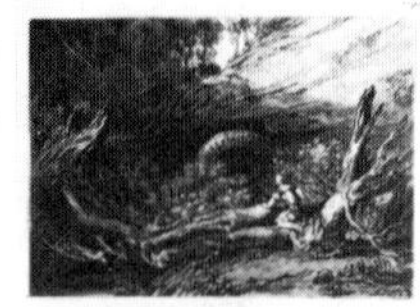
6 *Jason*

2

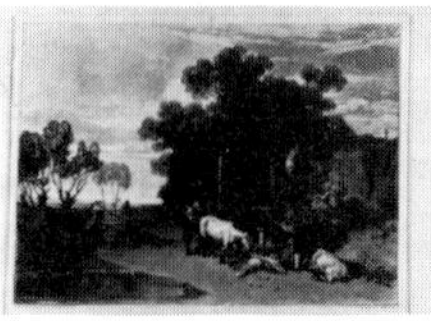
7 Straw Yard

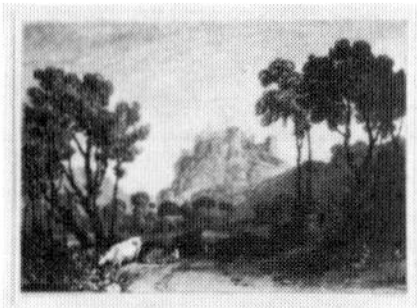
8 Castle above Meadows

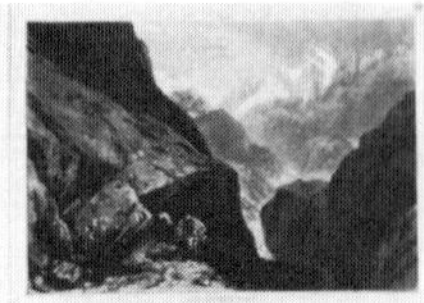
9 *Mt St Gothard*

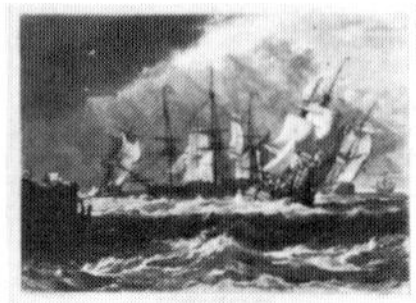
10 Ships in a Breeze

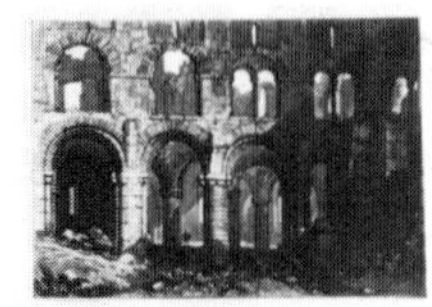
11 *Holy Island*

3

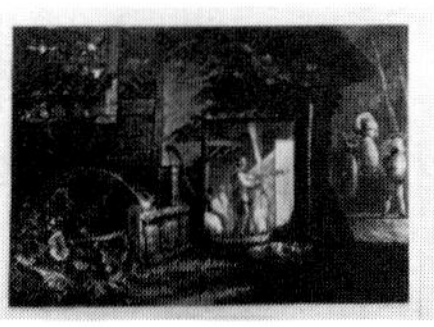
12 *Pembury Mill*

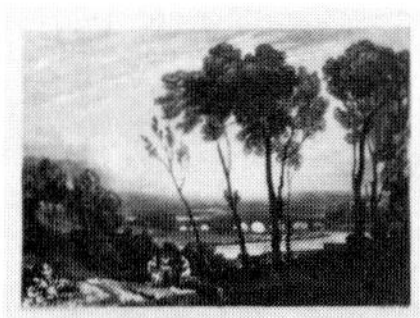
13 Bridge in Mid. Dist.

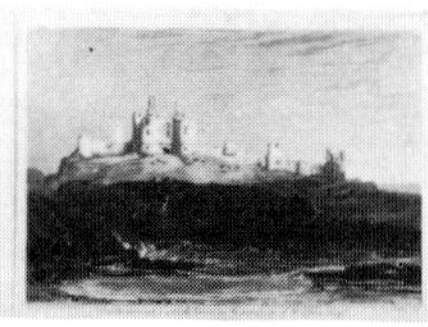
14 *Dunstanborough*

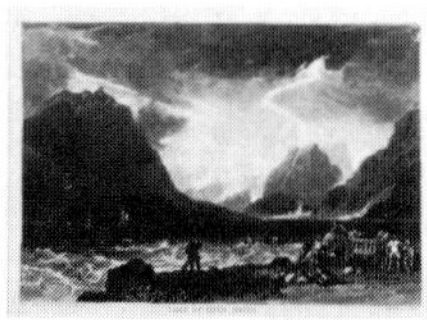
15 *Lake Thun*

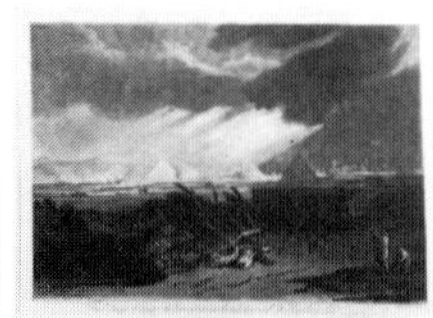
16 *5th Plague of Egypt*

4

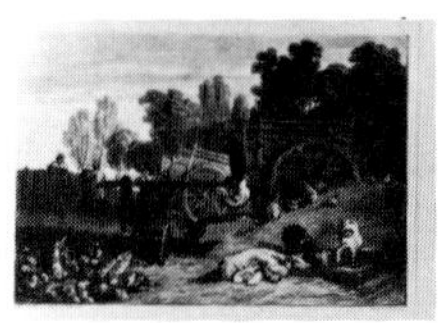
17 Farmyard

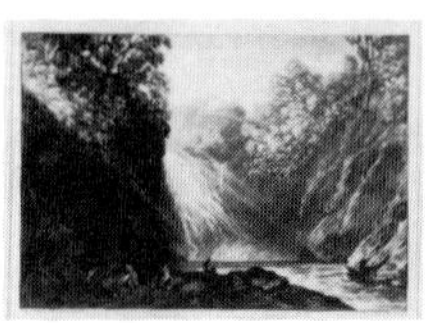
18 *Clyde*

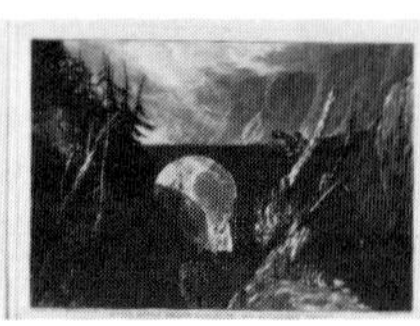
19 *Little Devils Bridge*

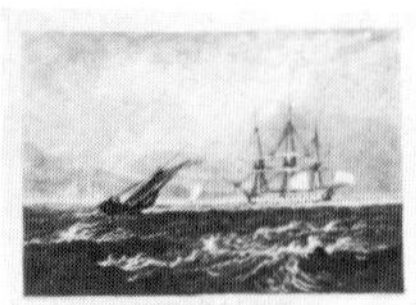
20 Leader Sea Piece

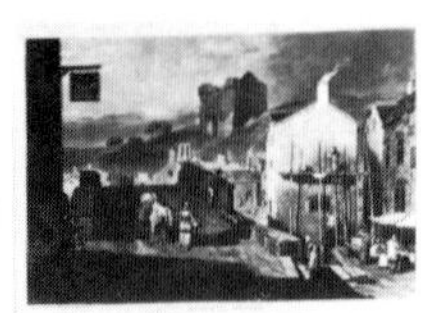
21 *Morpeth*

5

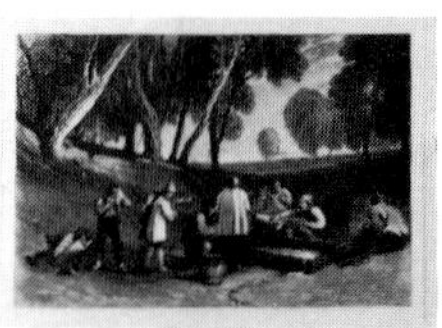
22 *Juvenile Tricks*

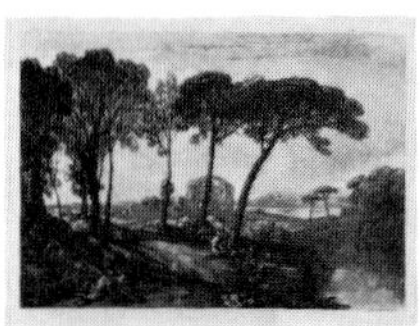
23 Temple of Minerva

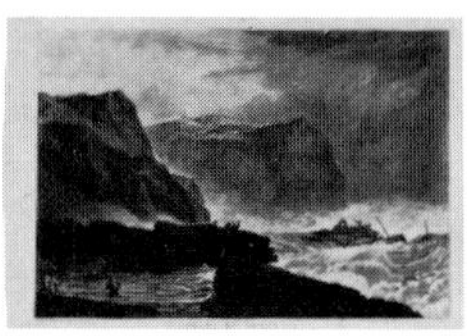
24 *Coast of Yorkshire*

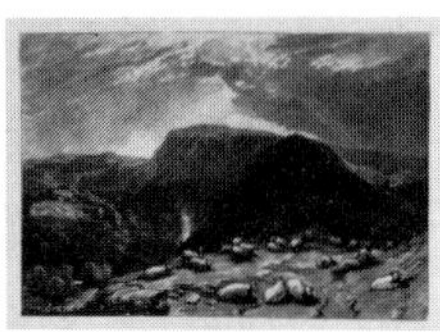
25 *Hind Head*

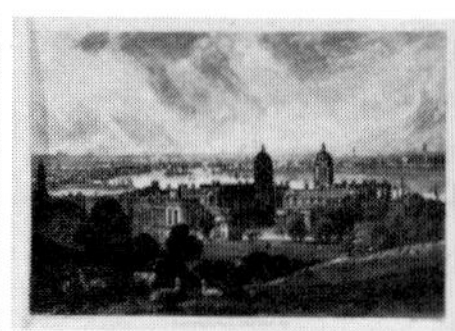
26 *Greenwich*

6

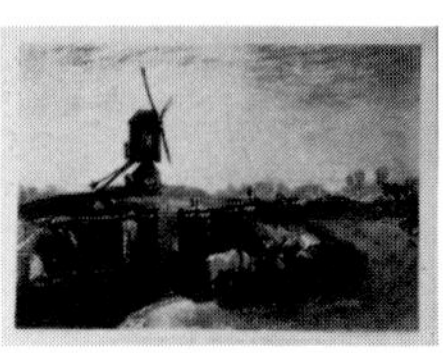
27 Windmill & Lock

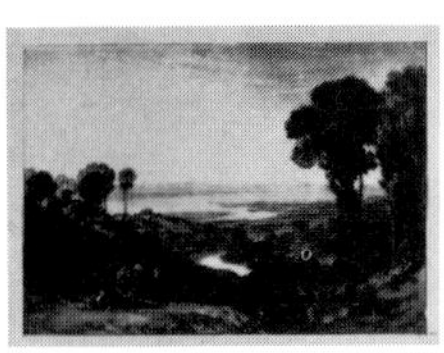
28 Severn & Wye

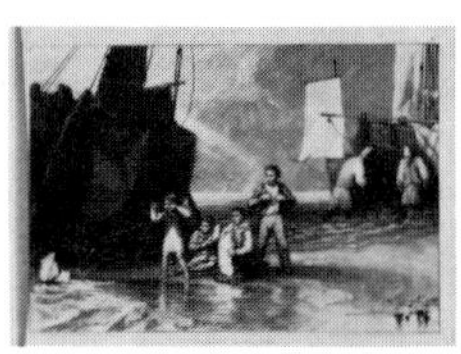
29 *Marine Dabblers*

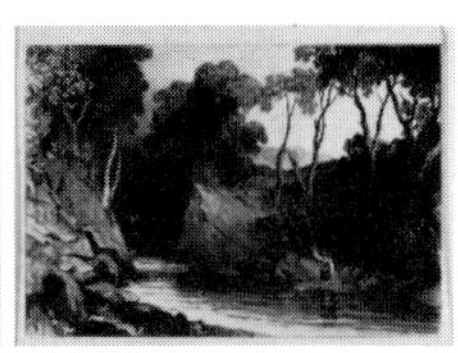
30 *Blair Athol*

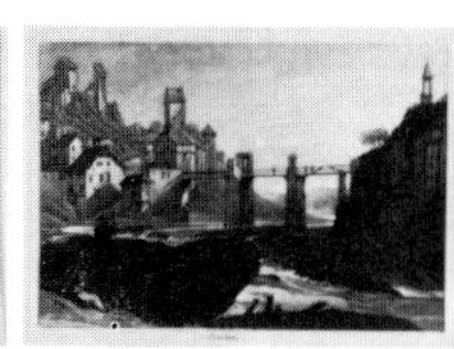
31 *Lauffenbourgh*

7

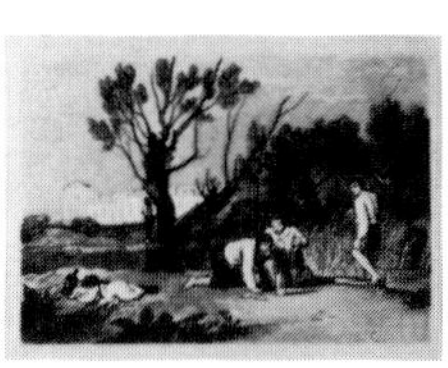
32 *Young Anglers*

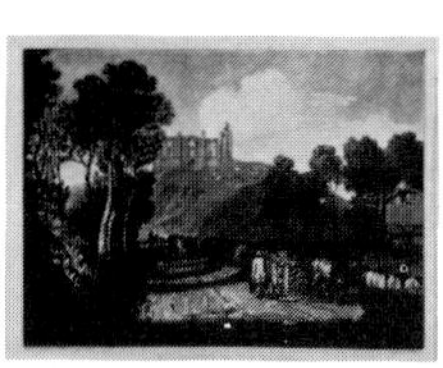
33 *St Catherine's Hill*

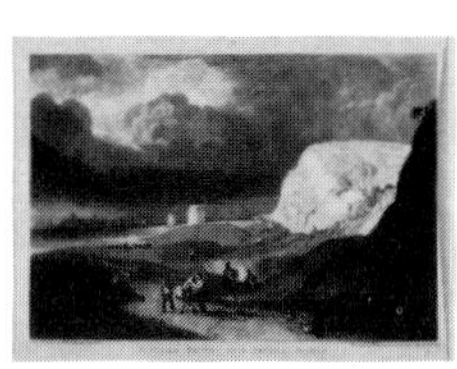
34 *Martello Towers*

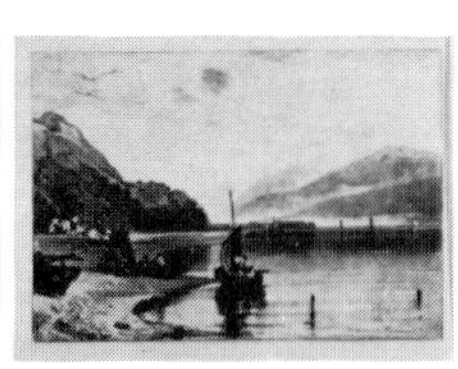
35 *Inverary Pier*

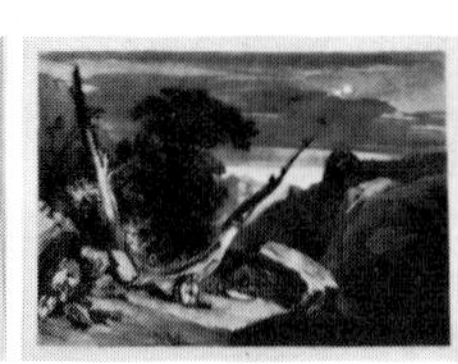
36 *Spenser's Fairy Queen*

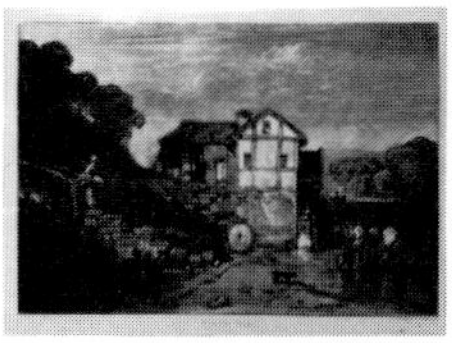
37 *Water Mill*

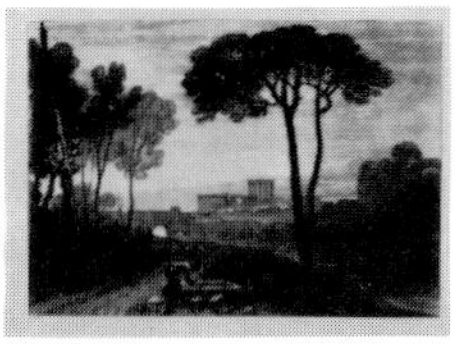
38 Scene in Campagna

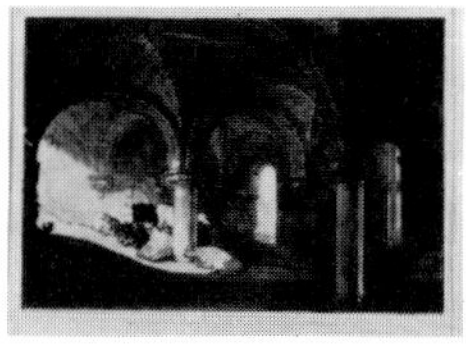
39 Kirkstall Abbey

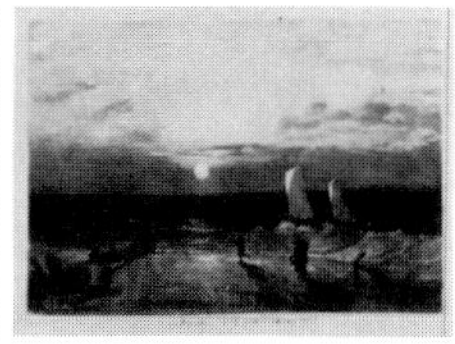
40 Mildmay Sea Piece

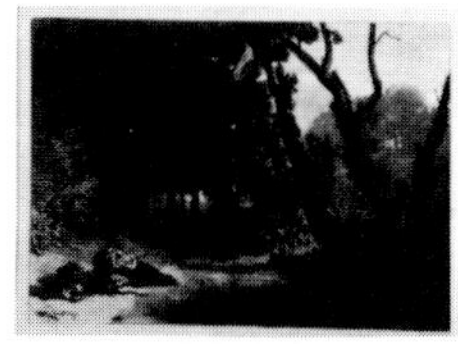
41 *Procris & Cephalus*

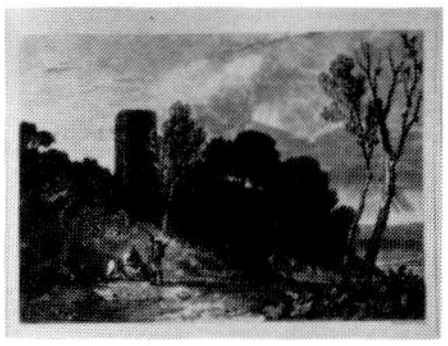
42 *Winchelsea*

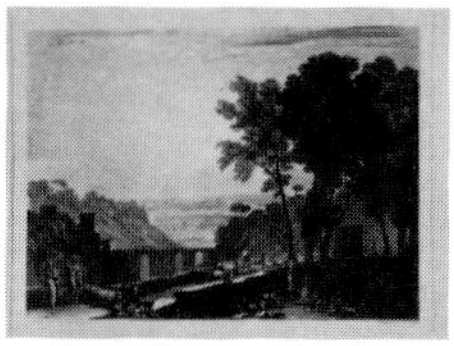
43 Bridge & Goats

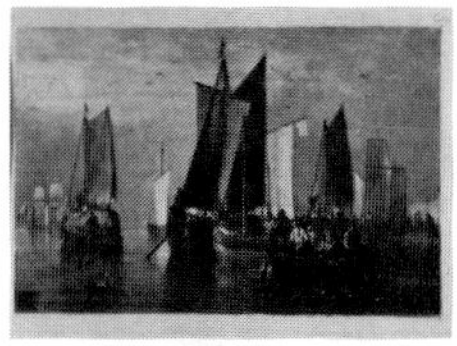
44 *Calm*

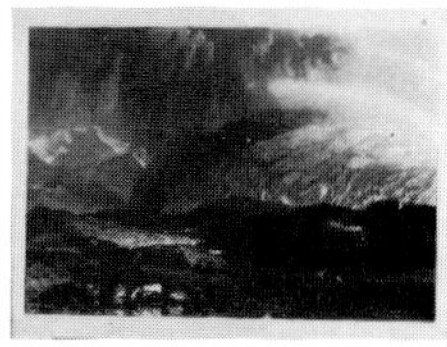
45 *Peat Bog, Scotland*

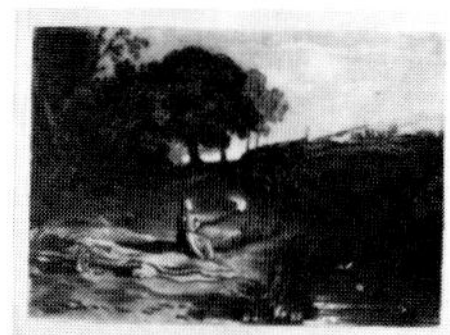
46 *Rispah*

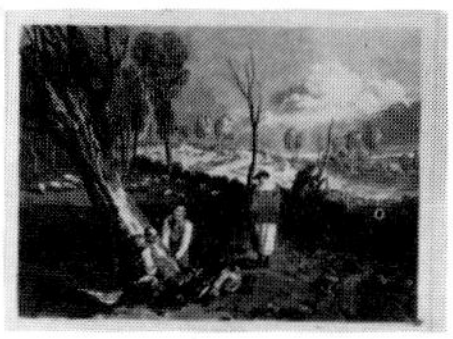
47 *Hedging and Ditching*

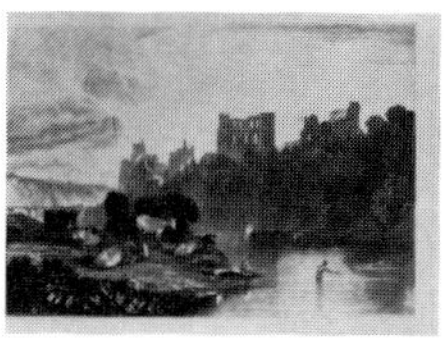
48 *River Wye*

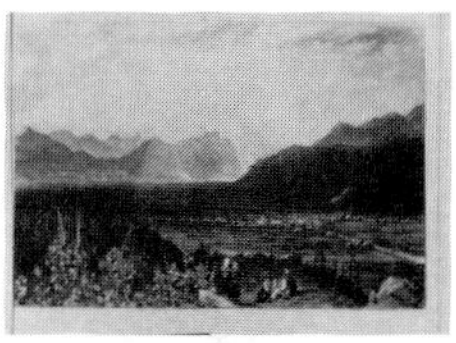
49 *Chain of Alps*

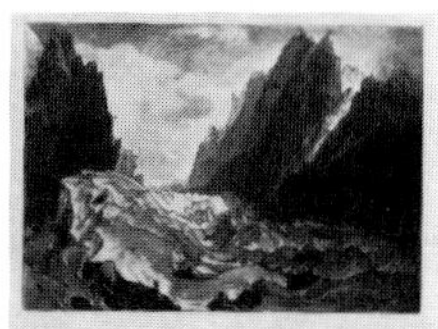
50 *Mer de Glace*

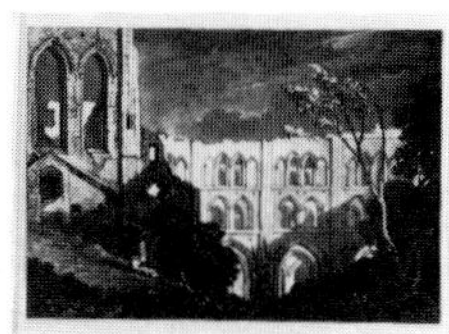
51 *Rivaux Abbey*

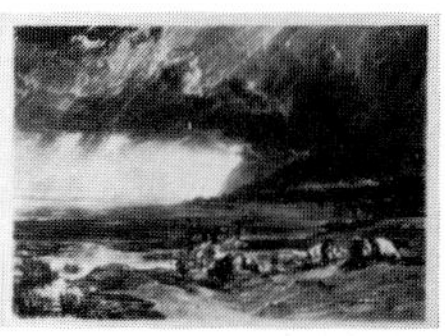
52 *Solway Moss*

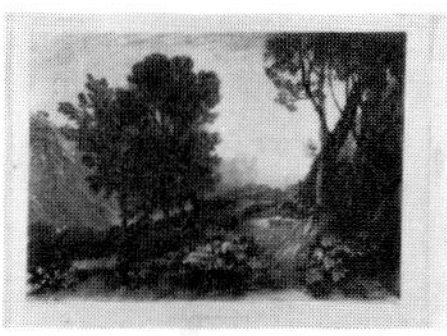
53 Solitude

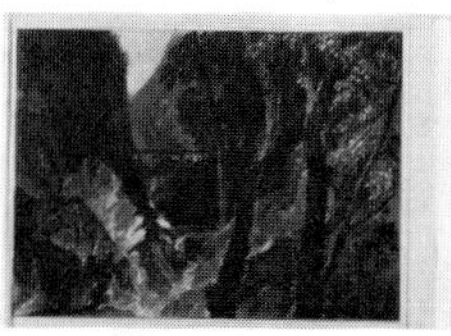
54 *Grand Chartreuse*

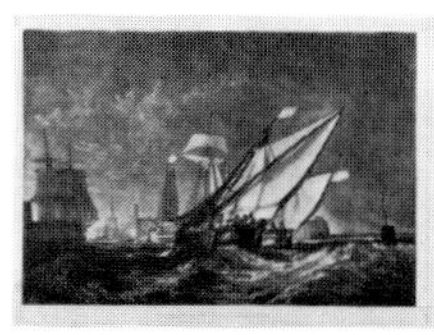
55 *Calais Harbour*

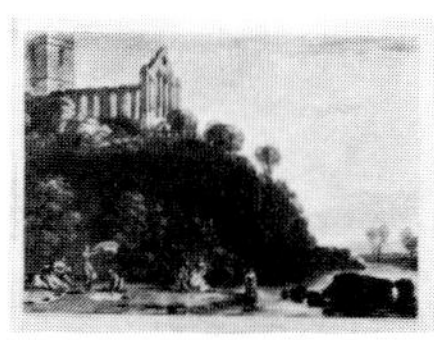
56 *Dumblain Abbey*

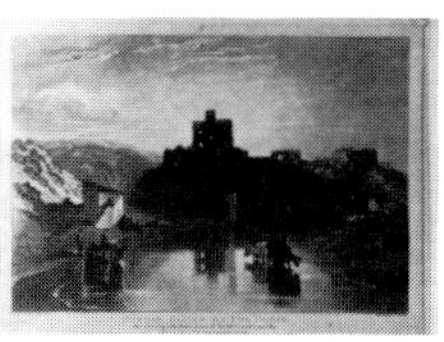
57 *Norham Castle*

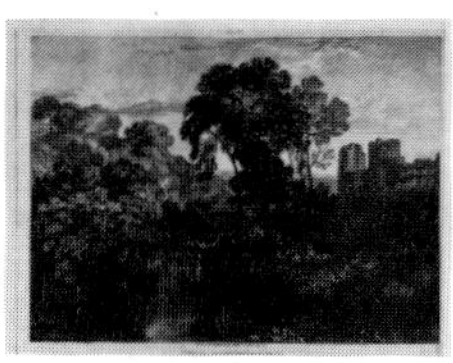
58 Berry Pomeroy

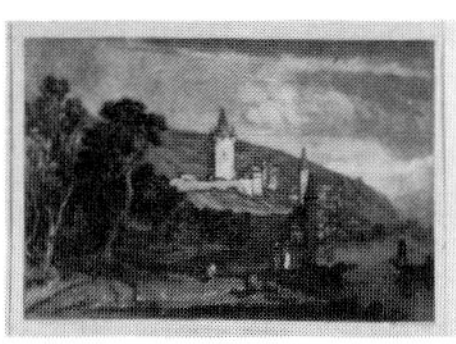
59 *Ville de Thun*

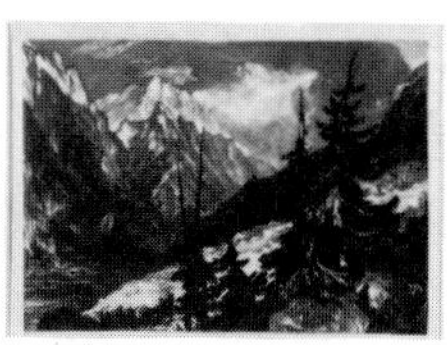
60 *Source of Arveron*

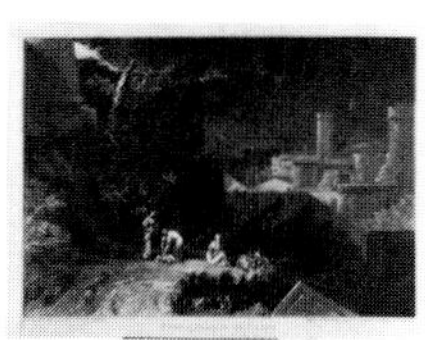
61 *Tenth Plague*

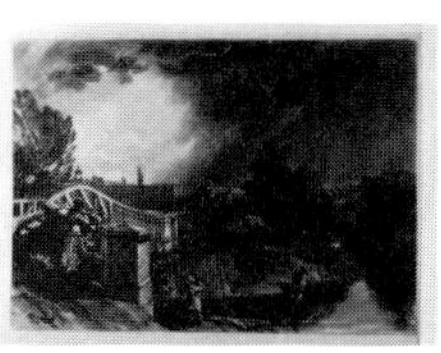
62 *Watercress Gatherers*

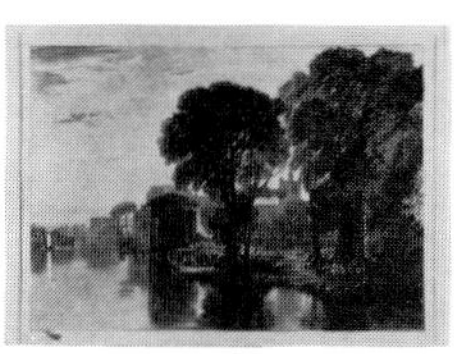
63 Isleworth

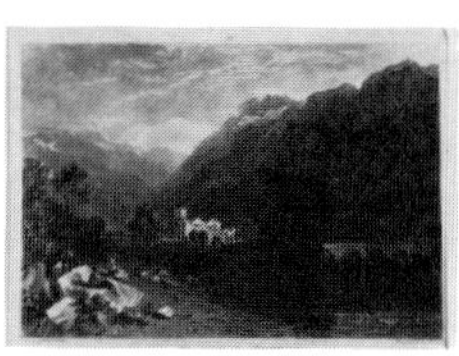
64 *Bonneville*

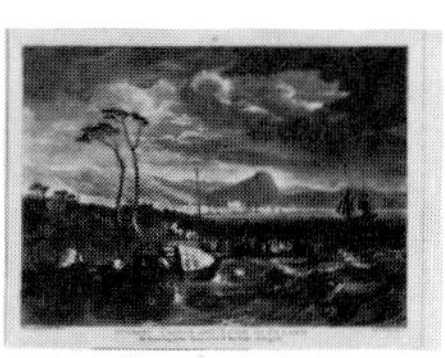
65 *Inverary Castle*

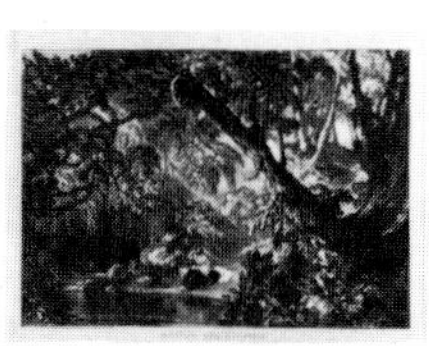
66 *Aesacus and Hesperié*

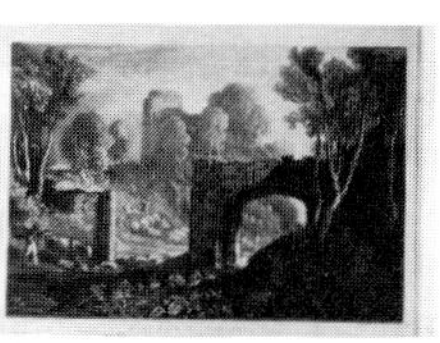
67 *East Gate*

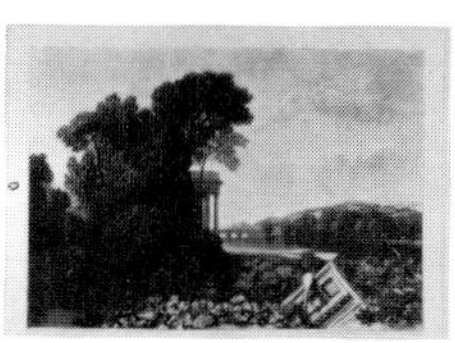
68 *Isis*

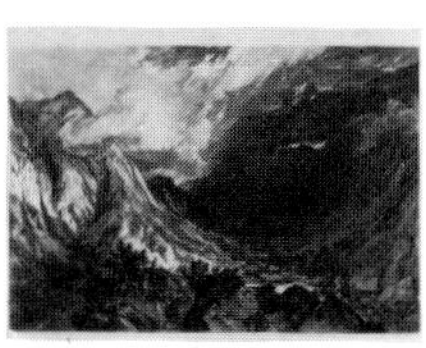
69 *Ben Arthur*

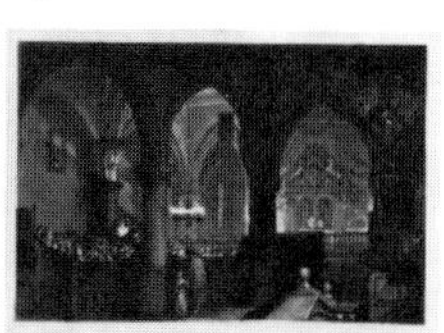
70 *Interior of Church*

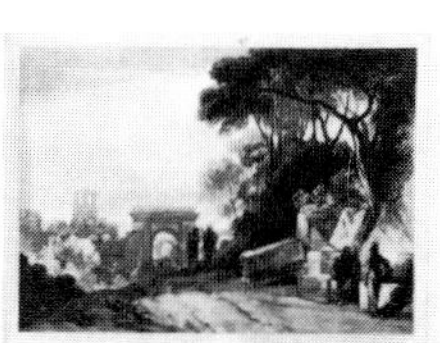
71 *Woman of Samaria*

Titles are abbreviated, with Turner's in italics. Plate 1 is the Frontispiece, reproduced on page 43.

INDEX

Aesacus and Hesperié 103
Akenside 56 60

Bach, J. S. 41
Bartolozzi, F. 29
Basire, James 30
Basle 47
Bell, C. F. 8
Ben Arthur 107 108
Berry Pomeroy 23 24 97
Blake, Wm 30
Bonneville 102 103
Boucher, F. 28
Boydell 7 15 18 19
Brentford 33
Bridge and Cows 44
Bridge and Goats 83
Bridge in Middle Distance 54 55
Brooke, Rev. Stopford 8
Burnet, John 32

Cadell, R. 96
Calais Harbour, Entrance of 3 95
Callcott, Sir A. W. 72
Calm 82 83 85
Castle above Meadows 50 51
Chain of Alps 86 88–9
Christ and the Woman of Samaria 110
Chryses 73
Claude Lorrain 7 12 15 16 18 19–21 113
Coast of Yorkshire 63 65
Cooke, W. B. 73 100
Cornwall 73
Cotman, J. S. 8
Covent Garden 32
Crome, John 31
Crowhurst 113 115
Cuyp 31

Danby, Sarah 9 72–3 77
Dawe, Henry 36 98
Dayes, Ed. 11
Devon 73
Devonshire Collection 19
Dolbadarn Castle 123
Dort 85 124
Du Fresnoy 50 123
Dumbarton Rock 115
Dumblain Abbey 95
Dunstanborough Castle 34 38–9 55

Earlom, Richard 7 12 15 19–21
East Gate, Winchelsea 106
Edwards, Ed. 11
Eton 2 113
Etty, Wm. 10

Fall of the Clyde 58 59
Farington 18 29 72
Farmyard with a Cock 58
Fawkes, Walter 63 72 99
Fibonacci 122
Fifth Plague of Egypt 57
Fighting Temeraire 125
Flint Castle 45 46
Frontispiece 8 43 91
Frosty Morning 105

Gainsborough 22 29 113
Geddes, Andrew 31
Gilpin, John 28 29
Gilpin, Sawrey 123
Girtin, John 33 34
Girtin, Thomas 33 49 50
Golden Section 60 110 122–5
Goya 113
Grand Junction Canal 69
Greenwich 36 63 66

Hamerton, P. G. 37
Hammersmith 34 72
Hastings Sketchbook 14
Hedging and Ditching 80 86
Hind Head Hill 49 63 65
Hindoo Worshipper See Plate 23
Hodgetts, T. 99

Interior of a Church 107 109
Inverary Castle and Town 103 104
Inverary Pier 76
Isis 107 108
Isleworth 103
Ivybridge 98

Jason 46 48
Junction of Severn and Wye 68
Juvenile Tricks 63 64

Kauffman, Angelica 29
Kingston Bank 118
Kirkstall Abbey 78 79 80

Lahee, S. 37 112
Landseer, Sir Edwin 10
Landseer, John 19 29 30
Lauffenbourgh 67 71
Leader Sea Piece 60 61
Le Prince 28
Leslie, Robert 10
Lewis, F. C. 33 34 35 82
Little Devil's Bridge 60
Little Liber 14 37 113
London from Greenwich 66
Lost Sailor 117
Lupton, Th. 37 92

Malton, Th. 28 29
Marine Dabblers 67 69
Martello Towers 73 75
Marylebone 73
Mer de Glace 86 90
Mildmay Sea Piece 80 81
Mill near the Grand Chartreuse 24 36 93
Moonlight at Sea 117
Moonlight on the Medway 118
Morpeth 62
Mt St Gothard 50 51
Munro of Novar 10

Napoleon 73
Narcissus and Echo 119
Norham Castle 35 96 125
North of England Sketchbook 38 80

Peat Bog, Scotland 36 84 85
Pembury Mill 54 55 80
Ploughing, Eton 2
Portsmouth 86
Poussin, N. 13 123
Procris and Cephalus 80 81
Pye, John 8 14 30 37

Raglan Castle: see Berry Pomeroy
Rain, Steam and Speed 125
Rembrandt 31 68
Reynolds, Sir Joshua 32 50 123
Reynolds, Samuel 107
Rievaulx 86 90 91
Rispah 84 85
River Wye 86
Rivers of England 37
Rome 18 78
Ruisdael 31
Ruskin, John 7 11 16 32 41–3 45 47 78 80

St Catherine's Hill 49 73 86
St Gothard sketchbook 99
Sandbank with Gypsies 119 120–1
Sandby, Paul 28
Say, Wm. 79 95
Scene in the Campagna 78 79
Scene on the French Coast 45 46
Scott, Sir Walter 76 96
Sheepwashing at Windsor 113
Ships bearing up for Anchorage 53
Ships in a Breeze 50
Shipwreck 7 36
Short, Frank 8 37
Smith, J. R. 15 32
Snowstorm, Hannibal 72
Snowstorm at Sea 125
Solitude 92 93
Solway Moss 36 92
Source of the Arveron 36 99
Spenser's Fairy Queen 66 73 74
Stonehenge at Daybreak 116
Stork and Aqueduct 116
Straw Yard 49
Sun rising through Vapour 85 124
Sunrise, Castle on a Bay 95
Sussex sketchbook 16

Temple of Minerva Medica 63 64
Tenth Plague of Egypt 99 100
Towne, Francis 86
Trimmer, Rev. 73
Turner, Charles 7 34 35 37 49 114
Turner Bequest 7 21

Ville de Thun 98 99

Walton Bridge 55 56
Water Mill 49 78
Watercress Gatherers 36 101
Watteau 50
Wells, W. F. 16 29 31
Wheeler, Clara 15
Wilkie, Sir David 63 113
Wilson, Richard 16 22
Winchelsea 82 106
Windmill and Lock 67
Windsor Castle 107 114
Woman with Tambourine 44 45

Young Anglers 73